Following HIM

WHEN I CAN'T SEE THE END OF THE ROAD

BARBARA FRANCIS

Following Him
When I Can't See the End of the Road

Published by
NewLife **Publications**
A ministry of Campus Crusade for Christ
P.O. Box 620877
Orlando, FL 32862-0877

Design and typesetting by Urick Design

Cover by Urick Design

Cover photo of Barbara Francis by Gary Nomura

Printed in the United States of America.

Unless otherwise indicated, Scripture quotations are from the New International Version, ©1973, 1978, 1984 by the International Bible Society. Published by Zondervan Bible Publishers, Grand Rapids, Michigan.

For more information, write:
L.I.F.E., Campus Crusade for Christ—P.O. Box 40, Flemington Markets, 2129, Australia.
Campus Crusade for Christ of Canada—Box 529, Sumas, WA 98295
Campus Crusade for Christ—Fairgate House, King's Road, Tyseley, Birmingham, B11 2AA, United Kingdom
Lay Institute for Evangelism, Campus Crusade for Christ—P.O. Box 8786, Auckland, 1035, New Zealand
Campus Crusade for Christ—9 Lock Road #3-03, PacCan Centre, Singapore
Great Commission Movement of Nigeria—P.O. Box 500, Jos, Plateau State, Nigeria, West Africa
Campus Crusade for Christ International—100 Lake Hart Drive, Orlando, FL 32832, USA

DEDICATION

To Bob

Husband
Lover
Partner
Cheerleader
Best Friend
Co-laborer in Christ

ACKNOWLEDGEMENTS

I am thankful for friends who prayed and helped me during the writing of this book:

My prayer team—You know who you are . . . I am blessed because of you.

My ministry partners—Since the summer of 1977, a team of financial backers have underwritten our ministry . . . how grateful I am for your generosity.

Jim Topmiller—For believing in me

Andrea Townsend—For all your help even when things took an unexpected turn

And finally, to my dear family—Bob, Bryan and Alison and Brooke . . .
you make my life

All proceeds from this book go the ministry of Campus Crusade for Christ.

Table of CONTENTS

"All I want to say to you is this, you are the Beloved. And all I hope is that you can hear these words as spoken to you with all the tenderness and force that love can hold. My only desire is to make these words reverberate in every corner of your being, you are the Beloved."

Henri Nouwen

FOLLOWING SHADOWS

Every family has one, and most of you will know immediately the name of that member of your extended family I refer to as the "irregular cousin." They don't speak properly, dress appropriately or eat politely. Consequently, no one wants to invite them to the traditional family gatherings—but you do. No one waits eagerly for their arrival, and everyone breathes a sigh of relief when they depart.

I always had a hunch that was how God felt about me. I didn't think I'd lose my salvation or get kicked out of His family altogether. I just thought that God was not very excited to have me around. I did not feel abandoned, just ignored. At candid moments I'd wish for just 30 seconds face to face with the Lord. I'd ask Him my heart's deepest question: "How do You really feel about me?" Then I'd wait to hear His words, to see His lips move, and to watch the look in His eyes. I stood in the shadows waiting for that moment.

It didn't happen in one moment, but over time, I have met Him in the pages of the Bible. He has taken my hand into His hands and whispered to my heart, "Hear My words, see My lips move, and watch the look in My eyes. I love you, Barbara, and I showed the depth of My love when I sent My dear Son. Step out of the shadows and look to Him. He is My gift of love to you."

My following became easier and more secure; the shadows were exchanged for the light of His love and the leading of His Son. Now, day after day, in the sunshine or in the rain, I have looked to Jesus. Although I am far from doing this perfectly, I am increasingly aware of how God really feels about me. He's thrilled I am in the family. And I'm not just a part of the extended family—I am a daughter, an heir, and seated on His lap.

- *How do you think God feels about you?*

- *Can you hear Him speak His love to you?*

My relationship with Christ Jesus has truly been life changing. Following Him has taken me down many avenues and each one has held wonderful discoveries that have drawn me closer to the Father's heart. My journey began even before I knew the Lord because He was gently leading me to Himself. The chapters in this book reflect aspects of my walk with the Lord.

So how about you . . .? Are you following Him or have you settled into the family role of an "irregular cousin?" Do you ever doubt His love or His timing or His leading? Are you longing to walk closer and grow in your understanding of God? I invite you to read the pages of this book with an awareness that we are walking together, and even when the going is rough and temptations to quit are great . . . keep going. We can reach our desired destination.

My prayer is that you'll be encouraged, as I have been, by the lives of these Biblical women. They have gone before us and left markers along the way to help us stay faithful on our journey until it leads us right to the throne room in heaven. There we will see His eyes sparkle and see His lips move and hear His voice say, "Welcome home, My beloved, My bride."

- *Consider where you are in your relationship with God.*

- *Reflect on where He has taken you.*

- *Prepare your heart to step out of the shadows.*

*"Only Jesus revealed that God is a Father of
incomparable tenderness, that if we take all
the goodness, wisdom and compassion of the
best mothers and fathers who have ever lived,
they would only be a faint shadow of the love and
mercy in the heart of the redeeming God."*

Brennan Manning
The Signature of Jesus

Avenue to
DISCOVERY

If you haven't already, let me invite you to think a rather
daring thought . . . you are deeply loved by God. I suspect,
for many, this may come as a shock. You scroll through
your mind the many things you have or have not done, do
the math, and it certainly doesn't add up to being loved by
anyone, much less by God. For others who may have had
some religious training in their background, "God loves you"
is a well-worn phrase from Sunday school but holds little
relevance in life today. But something in us wants to believe,
and still seeks real love—a love that will not fade, fluctuate,
or falter, no matter what we do.

- *Think back to your earliest memories of God.*

- *Remember your first longings for love,
  acceptance and belonging.*

I was well into my teens when I heard that God loved me. I had a vague memory of hearing, "Jesus loves the little children." But since I didn't see myself as a little child, I figured I'd missed the cut. Love had fallen on another, not me.

During my freshman year of college, everything changed. I was ambushed by the love of God in the person of Jesus Christ. I never knew that such a Lover existed, and if I'd dared to believe He did, I would never have expected He'd want anything to do with me. I was not religious and not very good at coloring inside the lines during my teen years. I tried reading the Bible once, thinking that would be a good place to search for God. I had opened it up and begun reading. I'd made it about 20 chapters into the book of Genesis and concluded, "This is NOT for me." That was the end of my Bible reading.

Later that same year at the University of Oregon, on a Friday night, some events took place and set into motion a whole series of changes that still have a ripple effect in my life today.

My high school boyfriend came to Eugene for a visit. You remember your first love . . . I was convinced he was my knight in shining armor and surely we would find our castle and live happily ever after. But that January visit proved to be the beginning of the end. It became very apparent that our relationship was based on a lot of nothing and was ending in a rather abrupt fashion.

He headed back to California, ready to consider what a friend had been telling him about a personal relationship with Jesus Christ. He decided to accept Him as his Savior.

Then he wrote me the dreaded "Dear Barbara" letter. He informed me that he'd become a Christian. When I received that letter a few days later, I flipped out. My own boyfriend had become a Jesus freak! So I decided to call him and tell him, in words best not used here, how upset I was. He listened as I ranted and raved. At the end of our conversation he said, "How can you say you don't want something you know nothing about? Read one of the first four books in the New Testament so if you do choose to reject Christ, at least you'll know who you're rejecting." I hung up! But his challenge did not go unfulfilled.

After a good cry that Friday night, I found a Bible and began in the gospel of Matthew. I was transfixed. Here was a Savior interacting with people like me . . . different culture, different slice of history, to be sure . . . but ordinary people—people with hurts, needs and cares. He moved to them, not away. He offered hope and healing. He was God with skin on. I was intrigued and had to know more. I had plans to go to a party on campus that night, an event that normally would have been a priority. But things were changing in ways I couldn't figure out. I left the gathering early because I could not get God and the Bible off my mind.

It was late Saturday night when I went to the Yellow Pages dangling near the pay phone on my dorm floor and looked up "Churches," ran my finger down the page until I hit the "Non-Denominational" section, and called the first one. I woke the pastor up and told him I wanted to become a Christian and asked if he could help. He assured me he could. The next morning I borrowed a bicycle and biked five miles across the town of Eugene to a small church where I was the youngest by about 200 years! The pastor, I later

13

found out, had stayed up the rest of the night to rewrite his message for me, the pagan college girl coming to church the next day. And it was well worth it. Through that message God opened my ears to hear that He loved me and wanted me to be with Him in a relationship filled with warmth, intimacy, and grace. It was almost too good to be true. I learned that sin kept me from experiencing this kind of a relationship and that the very reason Christ came was to do what I never could: pay the penalty for all the sin I knew was a part of my life. Now, I had a couple of choices: to accept this free gift of salvation or get back on my bike and forget the whole thing. I opted for the first one. I whispered a heartfelt prayer, telling the Lord I was a sinner and desperately wanted to be forgiven, changed and set on a new path. Guess what? He heard and answered my plea. The pastor was so excited that I had decided to follow Christ, he took me to lunch!

When I headed back to my dorm later that afternoon, two of my dorm mates stopped me, wondering where I had been because I looked different. But their kindness soon turned to anger when they realized how much my life was to change. They put signs on their doors stating, "Have you heard the good news? Jesus Christ is dead," and refused to even sit with me at meals. It was an incredibly lonely time. But God came to my rescue in the form of a young man I'd never seen before nor have seen since. One afternoon, as I approached the stairwell of my dorm, he stopped me and asked if I had become a Christian. I said yes, and he directed me to a Bible study that met on Sunday morning. That study was the beginning of my connection with the Christian community. I met a staff member with Campus Crusade for Christ who was used mightily by the Lord in my life.

In the weeks after all this happened, I headed home for spring break. It was the first time I'd seen my boyfriend since my decision for Christ. You can imagine his response when I told him all that had transpired. He was speechless. He had been praying for me, and now I was his first answer to prayer. Many things had to change in our relationship. But a year and a half later, that boyfriend and I were married. That was 28 years ago.

- *Consider where you are in your spiritual journey.*

- *Have you had a personal encounter with Jesus?*

As I sat in my fourth floor dorm room all those years ago, I had no idea where the road ahead was leading. I was embarking on an Avenue to Discovery—discovering who God is, discovering how to live in a way that brings Him pleasure and, most importantly for me, discovering just how much I am loved by God. He loves me without reservation, without limit, and without condition. And He loves you the exact same way. Jesus left the glory and perfection of heaven to come to earth as a man to rescue you and me from the pit the Bible calls sin. And I don't know about you, but I am so glad the Savior knew I was drowning in all my excesses, all my pride and prejudices, all my guilt and shame for past wrongs and current missteps . . . and came in love to save . . . *me*. I hadn't missed the cut after all.

So, where are you on the Avenue to Discovery? Many of you are still cautious about getting started. Jesus said, "I am the way, the truth and the life. No one comes to the Father except through Me" (John 14:6). It was when I came to know the Lord that I found real meaning, direction and purpose. A relationship with Him is the only way to begin the journey. He is the Avenue to Discovery. You can begin your journey just like I did. It is as simple as admitting your need for a Savior. All the good works in the world cannot make you fit for heaven (Ephesians 2:8-9). Just ask Him to come into your life, forgive your sins, and make you new from the inside out (John 1:12, Revelation 3:20). It is His pleasure to hear and answer that kind of prayer.

> • *Is it time to begin your excursion on the Avenue to Discovery through a relationship with the Lord Jesus?*

The first step on the Avenue to Discovery is simple, but the next steps require courage. Some begin well but drift. You may try a shortcut on the Avenue to Discovery and get lost. Perhaps you have a vague memory of what it was like to have a close, intimate walk with the Lord, but it's been a while. Like the sheep that wandered away from the fold (Luke 15:3-7), you've left the Shepherd for a million different reasons: the world's glitter caught your attention, guilt from a drastic mistake made you wonder if God withdrew His love, you've had a rebellious child, a loveless marriage, financial reversal, catastrophic illness, a deep longing left unmet, a busy life, or unbearable grief.

> • *What has been a primary cause for you to drift away from the Lord?*

> • *What draws you back?*

A biblical picture that takes my breath away is found in
Luke 15:11-24. It is the magnificent parable of the prodigal
son. If it's been a while since you've read it, you may want
to dust off a Bible and look it up. Beware, if you've been
spiritually cool—it may bring you to tears. It is such a
pristine portrait of the longing love of God the Father. Let's
think of this portion of Scripture as a three-act play.

Act I: The Son's Rebellion.
Act II: The Son's Repenting.
Act III: The Father's Restoring.

In Act I, we find the main character, only described as the
younger son, making a brash request of his father, "Give me
my inheritance!" He was ready to take his money and run for
the big-city life of wine, women and song. And leave he did.

In Act II, when the money ran out, so did the friends, fun
and frivolity. He ended up not only feeding pigs but actually
eating their food! You can be sure this occupation is not
on the "Top 10 Most Wanted Jobs for a Jewish Man." But
there's nothing like a little time at the lowest possible place
to bring one to his senses. You can almost see him hit his
head gently with the palm of his hand and say, "What
on earth has happened to my life! I thought I had all the
answers and could live life on my own apart from my father.
What a fool I've been. I am going right back and beg him
for forgiveness. I no longer deserve to be considered his son,
but maybe he'll accept me as a slave." It is a remarkable
turnaround and a real picture of repentance.

Act III opens with the father waiting for the son's return.
Day after day he'd walked to the edge of his estate, seeing
if there was a figure walking home. He'd done it constantly
since the day his son left so proudly. But today all his desires

were fulfilled. His boy was home! Listen how the Bible puts it: "While he was still a long way off, his father saw him and was filled with compassion for him; he ran to his son, threw his arms around him and kissed him." Unbelievable. No lecture, no spanking, and no withdrawal of affection. The son confessed his foolishness to his father, expecting to be sent to the slave quarters. Wrong again. The father exclaimed loudly, "**My son** has come home."

When we sin, confession needs to be made (1 John 1:9; Psalm 32) so our intimacy can be restored, but the security of the relationship as a son or daughter is never touched. If you find yourself playing the part of the prodigal son, it's time to head home with a prayer of repentance in your heart, anticipating a welcoming hug from your Abba.

Proceeding down the Avenue to Discovery always requires courage to change so we can become more and more like Jesus.

- *Quietly reflect on how the Lord has spoken to you.*

- *Tell Him in your own words what He means to you.*

DISCOVERY

Consider...

God's Word

> *"But I trust in your unfailing love; my heart rejoices in your salvation. I will sing to the LORD, for he has been good to me."*
>
> **Psalm 13:5-6**

> *"Yet to all who received him [Jesus], to those who believed in his name, he gave the right to become children of God."*
>
> **John 1:12**

God's Heart

> *"Behold, with great love have I chosen thee and made thee Mine, saith the Lord. Yea, My heart is drawn out toward thee, and I would minister to thee. I wait for thee to turn from everything else to Me alone. I want you to give Me all of yourself. I want the real you. The more you can bring to Me of your true self, the more I can give to you of My true self."*
>
> **Francis J. Roberts, *Come Away, My Beloved***

*Meditations
for the Journey
Discovery*

Following Him

*When I Can't See
the End of the Road*

20

*Singing* . . .

Discovering God's love leaves us speechless. Why would God choose me to be His child? An old hymn, written in 1860 by Anna B. Warner, comes to mind as we close our eyes and raise our voice in sheer amazement:

> *Jesus loves me! This I know, for the Bible tells me so, little ones to Him belong; they are weak but He is strong.*
>
> *Jesus loves me! Loves me still, tho I'm weak and ill, that I might from sin be free, bled and died upon the tree.*
>
> *Jesus loves me! He will stay close beside me all the way. Thou hast bled and died for me; I will henceforth live for Thee.*
>
> *Chorus:* **Yes, Jesus loves me! The Bible tells me so.**

*Praying* . . .

> *Lord, keep drawing me deeper into Your great heart of love. Thank You for finding me and wooing me to Yourself. I shudder to think where I'd be if You had not saved me. Help me to continue to discover more of Your will, more of Your truth, and more of Your heart. In Jesus' name,* **Amen.**

> *"We must accept finite disappointments, but we must never lose infinite hope."*
>
> **Martin Luther King, Jr.**
> ***Encyclopedia of Christian Quotes***

Avenue to HOPE

Hope is in short supply today. Most of us would run out of fingers and toes if we tried to count all the people, places and things that have let us down . . .

> . . . our friends
> . . . our spouse
> . . . our health
> . . . our job
> . . . ourselves

- *What would you add to the list?*

- *On a scale of 1 to 10 (1 being full of hope and 10 further away than you'd care to admit publicly), rate your hopefulness quotient.*

Jesus understands and welcomes the hopeless to draw near and find in Him all their deepest needs met. He extends His love to the abused, the forsaken, the divorced and the downcast. Aren't you glad? What a mess we'd be in if we had to be neat and tidy before we could have a relationship with Him. Remember His remarkable words in Matthew 11:28-30? "Come to me, all you who are weary and burdened [not put together and perfect], and I will give you rest [not a lecture about how you're not measuring up]. Take my yoke upon you and learn from me, for I am gentle and humble in heart, and you will find rest for your souls. For my yoke is easy and my burden is light." And so we come, limping and longing for a little ray of sun to shine in our dark places. Good thing He is the Light of the World!

- *Tell Him where you're limping.*

- *Feel His concern right at your point of need.*

There is a New Testament woman who caught my attention and grabbed my heart. She was in a helpless place. Rejected and scorned by society, friendless, penniless, and sick almost to the point of death. Helpless, yes. Hopeless, no. The hemorrhaging woman of Mark 5 could easily have allowed her circumstances to dictate her life and her faith, but they did not. She could easily have chosen to end it all through suicide, but she did not. She could have been chained to bitterness and could have given resentment permission to choke what little life was left right out of her, but she did not. She came instead to One who was hope personified. And that made all the difference. Let's follow her Avenue to Hope and glean lessons from her life that still speak today.

A LITTLE BACKGROUND

Jesus had just finished healing a demon-possessed man in the
region of the Gerasenes, on the southern tip of the Sea of Galilee.
He and His twelve disciples were now crossing by boat back over to
Capernaum, Jesus' home base during His ministry in Galilee. Some
believe it was in the hills around Capernaum that the Sermon on
the Mount was given. The people of this large city were accustomed
to seeing Jesus do many miracles. Matthew 4:23 records some
of what He did in the region: "Jesus went throughout Galilee,
teaching in their synagogues, preaching the good news of the
kingdom, and healing every disease and sickness among the
people. News about Him spread . . . and people brought to Him
all who were ill with various diseases, those suffering severe pain,
the demon-possessed, those having seizures, and the paralyzed,
and He healed them."

It isn't difficult to imagine the level of excitement on the shore
of the Sea of Galilee that day when news reached the townsfolk
that Jesus was on His way. The crowd was huge, crushing,
and waiting for another miracle. But it is difficult to imagine
the desperation of the man who was the first to greet Him,
Jairus. As one of the synagogue rulers, Jairus was a lay official
responsible for worship services, running the weekly school,
and overseeing the upkeep of the building. He was a respected
official in Capernaum. There are not many Jewish leaders named
among Jesus' followers but he was one, without question. Before
a word was spoken, Jairus fell flat on his face before Jesus, publicly
displaying his faith and humility. The nature of his request strikes
at the heart of anyone who loves children. "My little daughter is
dying. Please come and put your hands on her so that she will
be healed and live" (Mark 5:23). Luke's gospel adds that she
was his only daughter, 12 years of age (Luke 8:41). Without a
second thought Jesus went with him. But He was not to proceed

uninterrupted. Into that great throng slipped the unnamed woman. She was neither important nor noticed but certainly no less needy than Jairus.

HER HISTORY

There is not a lot known about this woman. No guess as to her age, her looks, or her family background. But the story, found in three of the four Gospels, does give us a few tidbits which, when woven together, make her come alive. We are told three significant details.

First, she had been bleeding for 12 years (Mark 5:25). Because of her bleeding, probably a chronic menstrual problem, she was declared by Jewish law to be "unclean" (Leviticus 15:25-27). This label excluded her from normal life, since anyone coming in contact with her would also become "unclean." It is hard to overestimate the physical, social, emotional and psychological repercussions of such a long-term illness. There would have been no aspect of her life left unaffected. Emaciated after bleeding for so many years, she would have been barely able to get around. Such a journey to Jesus would have been arduous at best. If she'd been engaged or married at one time, that arrangement would have already come to a not-so-sweet end. Physical intimacy was out of the question for an "unclean" woman. If she was a mother, she would have been barred from ever seeing her children again lest they, too, be considered "unclean." She would have been forced to live with other "unclean" people in a shantytown far away from the "clean" population. Worst of all would have been the effect all this had on her spiritual life. She could never go to the temple to worship or participate in the Jewish holidays. The sad picture of her is taking shape.

• *Acknowledge places of pain in your life.*

Secondly, we are told three times within ten verses of her
suffering (Mark 5:26, 29, 34). *Webster's Dictionary* defines
suffer as "to feel or endure pain, to bear loss or damage." Sums
it up pretty well, doesn't it? She'd lost it all and probably felt
like damaged goods. No one could know how much she'd been
through, how much abuse she'd endured for an illness she didn't
even know how she got.

• *Have you ever felt like this?*

Lastly, we discover that she had spent all her money in an
attempt to get better, but to no avail. She was "under the care of
many doctors and had spent all she had, yet instead of getting
better she grew worse" (Mark 5:26).

Each description of this woman is like a concentric circle of pain,
rejection and dejection. You'd think she'd just give up, give out,
give in. No way. She may have been helpless but her hope of healing
pressed her on to Jesus. I picture her hunched over, very tiny and
frail, fully covered with her tunic so as not to be recognized as
the "unclean" one. Her plan? She'd just tiptoe into this bustling
crowd on the way to Jairus' house, touch His garment, and slip
out the way she came in. No one would see, no one would know.
But she was sure it was the solution to the problem. "If I just touch
His clothes, I will be healed" (Mark 5:28). Her faith propelled her
on . . . past her fear, past previous disappointments and prejudice.
Where man had failed she believed Jesus would succeed. She was
on the Avenue to Hope and nothing would stop her now.

Her history and ours have remarkable similarities. We don't speak
her language, live in her part of the world, or perhaps even share
the same religious background, but we can identify with her pain
and loss.

• *What has robbed you of your life, dreams, plans and hopes?*

I've learned there is more than one way to hemorrhage.
Many suffer the consequences of abortion, rape, addictions
and debilitating illness. They've left you emaciated, too.
I have read—

> Pain. We all know what it tastes like. Whether its
> source is physical, emotional, mental or spiritual:
> Its interruption in our lives disrupts and reshapes. It
> intercepts our hopes and plans; it rearranges our dreams.
> It always leaves a mark. (source unknown)

• *Recall marks left on your life.*

We suffer in so many ways. Seen and unseen, big and little.
We seek cures, we spend fortunes on doctors, medicine, books
and seminars. It's not that it's wrong to seek help, but too often
such solutions can keep us from what we need most—a fresh
encounter with Jesus. He still waits for the helpless to come to
Him. He continues to invite all who have tried so many cures but
have only gotten worse.

In his book *The Applause of Heaven,* Max Lucado states our need:

> Admission of thirst doesn't come easy for us. False
> fountains pacify our cravings with sugary swallows of
> pleasure. But there comes a time when pleasure doesn't
> satisfy. There comes a dark hour in every life when the
> world caves in and we are left trapped in the rubble of
> reality, parched and dying.

Some would rather die than admit it. Others admit it
and escape death.

"God, I need help."

So the thirsty come. A ragged lot we are, bound together
by broken dreams and collapsed promises. Fortunes
that were never made. Families that were never built.
Promises that were never kept. Wide-eyed children
trapped in the basement of our own failures.

And we are very thirsty.

Not thirsty for fame, possessions, passion, or romance.
We've drunk from those pools. They are salt water in the
desert. They don't quench—they kill . . .

We're thirsty for a clean conscience. We crave a clean
slate. We yearn for a fresh start. We pray for a hand
which will enter the dark cavern of our world and do
for us the one thing we can't do for ourselves—make us
right again.

- ***Identify places in your life where you need a fresh
start.***

HER HEALING

The whole tone of the story changes from bleak to beautiful in
verse 27, "When she heard about Jesus . . ." When He is figured
into the equation, things always take an upward swing. It is
no different here. We really don't know how she heard about

the Lord. Perhaps a leper or a blind man from her unclean community had been healed and had returned to tell the story. But news had reached her about a healer, a Rabbi who touched the untouchables and did miracles never heard of in Israel.

- *Ponder and embrace the truths in Psalm 72:12-13. "For he will deliver the needy who cry out, the afflicted who have no one to help. He will take pity on the weak and the needy and save the needy from death."*

She'd muster the strength, risk her life and get to Him, even if it was the last thing she did. This took boldness, desperation and strong resolve. Hearing about the love and power of Jesus aroused her faith. Genuine faith always involves action. She took the initiative and made her way to the Sea of Galilee.

- *Consider what steps of faith need to be made in your life.*

Finally she reached Him. Each step—hearing, coming, and now touching—brought her closer to the One who would change her life. When you think about it, she didn't do very much. She just reached out her hand and touched His robe. But she did *something.* She would not settle for the status quo. That's where healing begins: when we decide that something's got to change and we go to the One who has the power to help. And help He did!

The faith in her touch brought immediate healing. Instantly she knew she was free from her suffering. For 12 years she'd reached out and found no cure. Now she was free, finally free.

• *Evaluate places you are in need of freedom.*

One of the Hebrew names for God is Jehovah-Rophe. It means
God, our Healer. Jesus, God in the flesh, spent a great deal of
His time healing the afflictions of men and women. It gives us
a peek into the heart of God and His compassion for our needy
state. But why, so many ask, doesn't God heal me . . . my MS, my
paralysis, my cancer, my fibromyalgia or my migraine? The list
could go on and on. I do not pretend to understand the mind of
God. But I do know that God can and does heal. He healed our
daughter, Brooke, from kidney disease when she was in fourth
grade. On the emotional side of healing, He has untied huge
knots of depression, self-hatred, and perfectionism in me.

• *Make a mental list of the ways the Lord has
healed you.*

God is God, and I am not! He knows what needs to be in my
life to most effectively conform me to the image of Jesus. It was
the apostle Paul, still hearing a clear "No" from the Lord in an
area he longed to have healed, who said, "I will boast all the more
gladly about my weaknesses, so that Christ's power may rest on
me. That is why, for Christ's sake, I delight in weaknesses, in
insults, in hardships, in persecutions, in difficulties. For when
I am weak, then I am strong" (2 Corinthians 12:9-10). That
may include things I do not like or understand. He is more
committed to our holiness than to our happiness. If we put
physical healing at the top of the list as the best way for God to
show up in a situation, then we may miss the myriad of other
ways He wants to work in our lives.

Glyn Evans, in his book *Daily with the King*, gives needed
perspective:

The life of victory begins, not with a sense of fullness, but with a sense of emptiness. Too often I am occupied with victory instead of being occupied with need. I will never develop strong, vibrant faith without a feeling of helplessness and sometimes despair . . .. People who are self-satisfied never have great faith.

God used this woman's 12-year affliction and trial as a tool to woo her down the Avenue to Hope, straight into His arms. She didn't know it yet, but He had far more in mind for her than stopping the bleeding.

* *What tool has He used in your life to draw you closer?*

HER HEALER

Jesus spoke only twice in this encounter with the bleeding woman. One was a question and one was a statement of blessing. There are delightful lessons waiting to be learned as we probe them both.

Remember the scene. Our female friend had made her way as discreetly as possible to the person of Jesus, just touched the hem of His garment, and was cured. Now, she hoped to simply evaporate into the crowd and be gone. But then the unthinkable happened. Jesus stopped, quickly turned around with His eyes searching the crowd and asked, "Who touched my clothes?" (Mark 5:30). So much for an anonymous escape! What was she to do? She was the only one who could answer His question. The entire procession to Jairus' house had come to a complete halt because of her touch.

But this probing question of Jesus was directed at the woman and sheds light on all the major players in the scene: Jesus, the disciples, the crowd and the woman. Jesus is full of healing, He is sensitive and responsive to the touch of genuine faith. He is ready to help not only the wealthy and influential, but the weak and unknown. I love that about Him. So, does His question indicate He really did not know what happened? I don't think so. He is God and knows everything. My guess is that He asked the question to use the incident as a teaching moment for everyone, including the woman.

So, what does this question reveal about the disciples? By now, they should have understood that Jesus wouldn't even have noticed something as trivial as His clothes being touched unless there were a more important matter at stake. But Peter's question reveals no awareness whatsoever that Jesus had more than the obvious in mind: "You see the people crowding against you . . . and yet you can ask, 'Who touched Me?' " (Mark 5:31). It was as if the disciples were saying, "Give me a break! How on earth can we answer that question?" They were clueless.

Jesus wasn't one to waste words or ask questions that made little sense. In time the disciples' spiritual discernment would be trained to know that something more was going on. That takes time in the presence of the Master, leading to a knowledge and familiarity with His ways. For now, perhaps, the disciples were still viewing life from a physical standpoint, unable to interpret the spiritual implications of the event.

In one sense, Peter was right. The crowd was smothering the Lord. Many of them had to have made physical contact with His garment. But only one was healed. So, we learn from the crowd that many can be around Him, listening to Him, following Him, even touching Him, yet never experiencing help at their deepest point of need. We must come to Him full of faith, with our specific need, believing that He can and will meet us in some way. It's the touch of faith that Jesus responds to.

And then there is our healed woman. Jesus' question brought her face to face with her healer. She fell at His feet, trembled with fear, and told Him the whole truth (Mark 5:33). I picture the crowd shocked that she was there. They all moved away for fear of being contaminated and deemed "unclean" themselves. All moved but Jesus. There, encircled with the townsfolk as an audience, He continued the healing that had only just begun. You see, she'd come in from behind, full of shame and guilt, only wanting her bleeding to stop. But Jesus wanted a face to face encounter to heal her broken heart and spirit. He wanted to love her and esteem her by acknowledging to all that an "unclean" woman had touched Him. It was not only "OK," it was part of His plan, and He proclaimed her healed. Through this public act He gave her recognition and respect, something Jesus made a habit of doing for women. Who touched His clothes? A humble and helpless one who is forever remembered for her genuine faith.

With whom do you most identify in this scene? One of the disciples—one who knows the Lord but is young and inexperienced in His ways? The crowd—familiar with His deeds, curious, ready to observe, but not desperate for personal revival? Or the woman—humble, eager to be near Him, and forever changed by the coming?

- ***Make personal applications to your life.***

Back to the story. Jesus then went on to bless the woman in front of the amazed crowd. "Daughter, your faith has healed you. Go in peace and be freed from your suffering" (Mark 5:34). He knew all along how much she had suffered! How understood and comforted she must have felt as she knelt at His feet.

- *Meditate on Psalm 145:14. "The LORD upholds all those who fall and lifts up all who are bowed down."*

- *Pinpoint a time in your life when you felt upheld by the Lord.*

He called her daughter, a name of endearment and intimacy. This is the only place in the New Testament where Jesus looked a woman in the eye and called her daughter. How loved she must have felt at that moment. This was beyond her wildest dreams . . . that God would call the "unclean" one daughter. He saw past the exterior, right to her heart of need and humility.

Then He acknowledged the role that faith had played in this miracle. Faith derives its value not from the one who expresses it, but from the object in which it rests. And hers rested firmly on the person of Jesus Christ. Max Lucado, in *The Applause of Heaven*, captures the essence of real faith:

> Faith is the conviction that He can and a hope that He will. Not too complicated, is it? Faith is the belief that God is real and that God is good. Faith is not a mystical experience or a midnight vision or a voice in the forest—it is a choice to believe that the One who made it all hasn't left it all. And that He stills sends light into shadows and responds to gestures of faith. Faith is not belief that God will do what you want. Faith is the belief that God will do what is right.

In the bleeding woman's case, the Lord did both what she wanted and what was right. She began on the Avenue to Hope needy and helpless. She had no idea that following Him would take her to a place of such love and esteem.

- *Put yourself into this narrative as the main character.*

- *Feel the Lord's love moving toward you, not away.*

- *Hear Him call you His dear daughter or son.*

Will you come to the Lord with your sufferings, disappointments and fears? You may feel ever so helpless, but please don't feel hopeless. Why? Because we have a God of hope, One who is very present in our times of need. Perhaps you are ready to embark on the Avenue of Hope. He awaits your arrival.

Meditations for the Journey
HOPE

Consider . . .

God's Word

> May the God of hope fill you with all joy and
> peace as you trust in him, so that you may
> overflow with hope by the power of the
> Holy Spirit.
>
> **Romans 15:13**

> The LORD is good to those whose hope is in
> him, to the one who seeks him; it is good to
> wait quietly for the salvation of the LORD.
>
> **Lamentations 3:25-26**

God's Heart

> I am, O God, a jumbled mass of motives. One
> moment I am adoring You, and the next I
> am shaking my fist at You. I vacillate between
> mounting hope, and deepening despair. I am
> full of faith, and full of doubt. I want the
> best for others, and am jealous when they get
> it. Even so, God, I will not run from Your
> presence. Nor will I pretend to be what I am
> not. Thank You for accepting me with all my
> contradictions.
>
> **Richard Foster, *Prayers from the Heart***

*Meditations
for the Journey
Hope*

Following Him

*When I Can't See
the End of the Road*

36

Singing . . .

O God, Our Help in Ages Past

*O God, our help in ages past, our hope for
years to come, our shelter from the stormy
blast, and our eternal home.*

*Under the shadow of Thy throne still may we
dwell secure; sufficient is Thine arm alone,
and our defense is sure.*

*O God, our help in ages past, our hope for
years to come, be Thou our guide while life
shall last, and our eternal home.*

Isaac Watts, 1674-1748

Praying . . .

*You are my God of hope! Please write this
truth on my heart, Lord; I am so forgetful. My
hope is drained when people disappoint me. My
hope dissipates when You don't act like I think
You should. So, I say it again, You are my
God of hope. How I praise You that You never
change!*

> *"Happiness can be found neither in ourselves nor in external things, but in God and in ourselves as united with Him."*

Pascal
Source Unknown

Avenue to DESIRE

OK, so the fourth grade was not my best year. It started out in the usual way, meeting new friends, going to school, nothing out of the ordinary. That was until I met Oliver Troster. I was smitten! He was the cutest boy I had ever seen and the only thing I could think about. If only he had the chance to get to know me, I was sure he would feel the same way, too.

Then came Wendy Petersmeyer. Tall, slender, long blonde hair, dressed great, you know, all the stuff that leaves the rest of us in the "average" category. That was the end of my dreams for Oliver.

He was my "first love." Probably more like puppy love or a pre-teen crush. Retrospectively, I'm grateful I got over it. But there is one love that I don't ever want to get over—my love for Jesus.

- *Analyze your love for the Lord . . . is it fresh or fading?*

On the Avenue to Desire we need to reflect on our love for the Lord and ask some soul-searching questions:

> What are the deep longings of your heart?
> What are you earnestly striving after?

I suppose there are as many answers as there are readers of this book. Financial security, meaningful relationships, a deepening walk with the Lord, healing of emotional wounds or physical afflictions. These are probably included on many of our " wish lists."

Judith Viorst, in her humorous book *How I Got to Forty and other Atrocities*, introduces us to a young man whose main goal is to be in charge of the world. Truth be told, it is the hidden desire within many of us! Here are a few of the changes he'd make:

> If I were in charge of the world
> I'd cancel oatmeal,
> Monday mornings,
> Allergy shots.
>
> If I were in charge of the world
> There'd be brighter night-lights,
> Healthier hamsters, and
> Basketball baskets forty-eight inches lower.
>
> If I were in charge of the world
> You wouldn't have lonely.
> You wouldn't have clean.
> You wouldn't have bedtimes.
> Or "don't punch your sister."
>
> If I were in charge of the world
> A chocolate sundae with whipped cream and nuts
> Would be a vegetable.
> All 007 movies would be G.

And a person who sometimes forgot to brush,
And sometimes forgot to flush,
Would still be allowed to be
In charge of the world.

• ***You may never be in charge of the world, but what
in your life would you change if you could?***

One thing I'd change if I had the chance is the tendency
within each of us to lose our first love for Jesus. We begin our
relationship with God with great hope of a fine finish. But with
work, family and the million and one things that need to be
done to live, He gets lost in the shuffle. Think for a moment
what our lives would look like if the Lord were allowed to play a
more central role. What if our sometimes-splintered, distracted
and inconsistent focus on our wonderful Lord were changed? I
daresay that every aspect of our lives would be affected. Our
personal walk with Him would be authentic and tender. Greater
love, forgiveness and grace would characterize our family life.
Certainly, we would be more spiritually mindful in the workplace
and even during our free time.

• ***Consider if you've lost your first love.***

My own journey as been far from perfect. I have stumbled and
fallen many times, but what draws me back is His love. Some
of my deepest desires are to know the Lord and have Him
increasingly a part of every facet of my life. I've sensed that God
has me on an Avenue to Desire. It is on that avenue where He
deepens my soul's hunger and thirst for Him and Him alone.
Perhaps that's why I am so intrigued by the women in the Bible,
because they teach me about how this desire is sparked and how
it is fanned into a full flame of love for God.

- *List some ways your life would be altered if Jesus
  were at the center.*

- *Think about what Colossians 3:1-2 says. "Since,
  then, you have been raised with Christ, set your
  heart on things above, where Christ is seated at
  the right hand of God. Set your minds on things
  above, not on earthly things."*

A galvanized gaze on Jesus and our hearts set on that which
pleases Him are what our inner person longs for, aren't they? I
think that's why I am so attracted to one woman who will lead us
down the Avenue to Desire. She is a delightful, biblical example
of one who started strong and went long in her walk with her
Lord. She wasn't flashy, competitive or overbearing. In fact, we
rarely hear her speak. She was simple, focused and determined.
Mary of Bethany exudes a quiet confidence and a contagious
devotion for her Lord.

- *Ask the Lord to teach you in very personal ways as
  we look into Mary's life.*

Just in case you've not heard much about Mary of Bethany, let
me give you a little needed information. The Bible identifies her
only as Mary, sister to Martha and Lazarus. No last name and no
other physical descriptions are given. Bethany, her hometown,
was a village on the eastern slopes of the Mount of Olives,
about two miles from Jerusalem. Jesus often returned to His
friends' Bethany home to find rest and refreshment after being
in Jerusalem. Many scholars believe that Mary's family was a
prominent one in Bethany because in John 11:1 it is referred to as
"the village of Mary and her sister Martha." Mary is best known
for her love for the Lord. It is her character that shines most
brightly from the New Testament accounts of her.

HER PASSION

"Passion" is a hot buzzword in Christian circles today. We see it in the titles of books and sermons, displayed on CD covers, and we hear it stressed in the lyrics of songs we sing. Nothing wrong with that. We could all use a little boost in the passion department. But what does it look like? How do we get it into our lives? Well, if a picture is worth a thousand words, we have a gorgeous portrayal of passion in each encounter with Mary. We will begin in John 12. An ecstatic celebration was going on in a home in Bethany. Do you remember why? Lazarus had just been raised from the dead! Mary and Martha, just hours before, had been overcome with grief and sorrow. But now it was time for feasting and joy. Lazarus, Jesus and the disciples were gathered around the table, Martha was serving a meal, and Mary was looking for a way to express her profound gratitude to the Lord.

In verse 3 we read, "Mary took about a pint of pure nard, an expensive perfume; she poured it on Jesus' feet and wiped his feet with her hair. And the house was filled with the fragrance of the perfume." Spikenard is aromatic oil extracted from an East Indian plant. Some scholars have suggested that it was worth a year's wages and may have been a part of Mary's dowry. Her act was a full, rich expression of her love and thanks. In this culture it was considered improper for a woman to take her hair down publicly, but here it was clearly a very personal expression of tenderness and humility.

She just had to do something for Him, something that could begin to express all she felt inside. He'd been there when she had needed Him most . . . at her darkest hour of grief. In the previous chapter, prior to raising Lazarus from the grave, Jesus had come to Bethany only to find Lazarus already dead. He had done that on purpose to show the glory of God (John 11:4). But Mary hadn't known that then. She'd been crushed and seeking answers as to why Jesus had not come sooner. She had known He could have prevented the whole tragedy. All she'd been able to do was throw herself at His feet and weep . . . her brother was dead and her heart was broken. He had not lectured her on her lack of faith. He had wept with her. In her sorrow, He had been her comfort. In her confusion, He had been her answer (John 11:32-33). And before long He'd given back to her what she had never dreamed possible, her brother. Now, the very least she could do was give Him the very best she had.

- *Think about a time when the Lord has met you in a dark place.*

- *Meditate on 2 Corinthians 1:3-4. "Praise be to the God and Father of our Lord Jesus Christ, the Father of compassion and the God of all comfort, who comforts us in all our troubles."*

- *Pause and pray. Thank God for being YOUR comforter in sorrow, YOUR answer in confusion.*

Lavish love and true worship—what a scene. It seems Mary understood, even better than the disciples did, what lay ahead for Jesus. He commented on her sensitivity when He said that the perfume was to be used for the day of His burial (John 12:7). He'd been telling His men for a year and a half that death waited in Jerusalem, but they never really made the connection the way Mary did. Here she ministered to the needs of the Lord by loving, giving, serving and sacrificing. And the fragrance of her sacrifice filled the whole house. It was an aroma of devotion.

The first stop on our Avenue to Desire is a Love Check-up. How is your love for Jesus these days? Measured or measureless? Lavish or lacking? I learn from Mary that desire is deepened when we give our best to the One who has given His best for us. I am struck by her generosity to God and the selfless way she worshiped. It was all about Him and little about her. It reminds me of what John the Baptizer said in John 3:30 when some of his disciples thought Jesus was getting a little too much attention, "He must become greater. I must become less." Such a determined focus on the Lord is one way our first love for Jesus is maintained and expanded.

I am quite convicted when I read Charles Spurgeon's questions:

> Think of what His love has brought you—justification, adoption, sanctification, eternal life. The riches of His goodness are unsearchable. O, how matchless is the love of Christ! Shall such a love as this receive only half our heart? Shall it have a cold love in return? Shall Jesus' marvelous lovingkindness and tender care meet with faint response and delayed acknowledgment?

- ***Do you give your best to Jesus?***

- ***Does He have your whole heart?***

Amazingly, not everyone thought Mary's act was such a grand idea. The story, recorded in three of the four gospels, shows the disciples reprimanding her for giving such an extravagant gift. Mark's account tells us that "they rebuked her harshly" (Mark 14:5). Matthew says that "they were indignant" and even suggested that the perfume should have been sold and the money given to the poor (Matthew 26:8). Jesus consistently helped the poor, but this moment was different. He was hours away from death. Mary's lavish and unrestrained love was greeted with a sneer by the 12 disciples. Did her devotion bring to light their lack? The fragrance of nard was pleasing to Jesus but a sign of foolish waste to others.

Have you ever been criticized for your love for Jesus? It's
happened to me on many occasions. When my husband, Bob,
and I decided to go into fulltime vocational ministry, we were
met with considerable opposition from a variety of people. Not
everyone thought it was a grand idea. They felt we'd gotten "too
carried away with this religion thing" and should calm down a
bit. They believed we were wasting our lives and our potential
and would probably end up penniless. They couldn't understand
the nature of God's call on our lives. His extravagant gift of
eternal life called forth from us a lavish response. Not just once,
but over and over. Now that will look different in every life. But
if you get serious on your Avenue to Desire, you may encounter a
bit of criticism along the way.

- *What is your lavish response to Jesus' gift to you?*

- *Recall times when you've felt judged for your love
for Jesus.*

The disciples may have misunderstood Mary's act, but Jesus didn't.
He came to her defense. Listen to how Mark 14:6-9 puts it:

> "Leave her alone," said Jesus. "Why are you bothering
> her? She has done a beautiful thing to me. The poor
> you will always have with you, and you can help them
> any time you want. But you will not always have
> me. She did what she could . . . I tell you the truth,
> wherever the gospel is preached throughout the world,
> what she has done will also be told, in memory of her."

Imagine that—God saying thank you to Mary, recognizing that
what she had done was a beautiful thing. The disciples may have
blown off her devotion as a waste, but not Jesus. He promised
her what He promised no one else, that her action of devotion

would be linked to the preaching of the gospel to the nations . . .
in memory of her. Her simple act of love was a foreshadowing of
what Jesus would do on the cross. I wonder how she felt when He
said that?

- ***What beautiful thing have you done for the Lord
lately?***

- ***Hear His words of thanks in your heart.***

The second stop on our Avenue to Desire is a Commitment
Check-up. Will we go the distance with the Lord? Do we have
an undistracted devotion? I learn from Mary's life not to shrink
even when criticism strikes. Some of my favorite people in the
Bible are ones who showed unusual tenacity in their walks with
the Lord. Noah, Abraham, Moses and Joseph, just to name a
few. All had reasons to quit. Noah built a huge boat miles away
from a body of water. Abraham didn't have any children yet was
told he'd be the father of many nations. Moses was to rescue
a people from the strongest nation on earth using a shepherd's
staff. Joseph was sold into slavery by his brothers, accused of
rape by Potiphar's wife, and forgotten in a prison by the king's
cupbearer. Yet he never showed signs of bitterness toward God.
The common denominator: commitment. They all were well
along the Avenue to Desire, learning to love the Lord with all
their might and stay the course no matter what.

- ***Pray about your dedication to the Lord.***

- ***Pinpoint some distractions to devotion.***

William Paulsell gives some helpful insight:

> It is unlikely that we will deepen our relationship with
> God in a casual or haphazard manner. There will be
> great need for some intentional commitment and some

reorganization in our lives. But there is nothing that will enrich our lives more than a deeper and clearer perception of God's presence in the routine of daily living.

- ***Decide to go deeper with the Lord.***

- ***Detail what that will look like.***

HER PLUMB LINE

This picture of passion from Mary's life is a snapshot from one of the last times we see her in the New Testament. I want to know how she ended up in such an honored yet humble position. For my answer I head to Luke 10:38-42:

> As Jesus and his disciples were on their way, he came to a village where a woman named Martha opened her home to him. She had a sister called Mary, who sat at the Lord's feet listening to what he said. But Martha was distracted by all the preparations that had to be made. She came to him and asked, "Lord, don't you care that my sister has left me to do the work by myself? Tell her to help me!"

> "Martha, Martha," the Lord answered, "you are worried and upset about many things, but only one thing is needed. Mary has chosen what is better, and it will not be taken away from her."

This is such a delicious section of the New Testament, full of insight that makes it applicable to our lives today. Jesus and His men were in Bethany and stopped by Mary and Martha's for a quick visit with His friends. Both women were serving the Lord in their own way. Martha invited Him in and was doing household things: cleaning, cooking, and preparing. She was involved in similar activities in the John 12 passage we've already considered. But during this visit there were some problems with Martha's attitude behind her activities. Poor Martha has taken a lot of hits over the years for her behavior in this portion of Scripture, so let's cut her some slack. Probably thirteen people had just shown up at her house for a meal, and there was no shortage of things to get done. Food had to be cooked, the table needed setting, and maybe she hadn't picked up the house from the night before. Most can relate to her distraction with the preparations. One thing she did right was taking her concern to Jesus. But the two things she did wrong were accusing Him of not caring about her and then proceeding to order God to do something about it . . . and make it snappy!

• *All Marthas, raise your hand.*

So, what was the problem that had Martha's "undies in a bundle?" Mary had the audacity to be sitting and doing absolutely nothing while Martha was running around like a chicken with her head cut off, that's what! Here is where it really gets good. The fact that the Lord answered Martha shows just how much He cared. Then He calmly and lovingly corrected her by telling her the truth about herself that, if left untold, would lead to a miserable life. Bottom line, she was worried and upset about many things; thus, she was distracted from Him. That's the main lesson Jesus had for Martha. Then He told her the truth about the situation: She was missing out on the best because she had wrong priorities. God was in her living room and she was in the kitchen. What's wrong with this picture?

All right, here's my confession. I am a Martha. I am queen of distractions. Good distractions, noble detours. But, like Martha, they take me the wrong way, away from Jesus. I need that same correction. I can get confused about who is to have first place in my life. It is the first step toward loss of first love, so I want to really listen to the Lord's kind rebuke and take it to heart.

- *Remember a time when God told you the truth about yourself or your circumstance.*

- *Did He use a person or His Word?*

- *Decide if there are some changes that need to be made in your life.*

Mary, criticized again for her devotion, had chosen the best. The Lord came to her defense again. She was quiet and drinking in His every word. Now, in this culture, sitting at His feet was no place for a woman. At a rabbi's feet was where his disciples sat—male disciples. God's choosing to include this bit of information in His Word gives us insight into the way He feels about women. Women have every right to learn and grow as do men. His Word and being in His presence are for everyone. All genders, all races, all nations. Isn't that a thrilling thought?

We also learn from Jesus' commendation to Mary that listening to Him is to be our number-one priority. Why? Because His Word is the plumb line for living. A plumb line is a small mass of lead or other heavy material suspended on a string. It is used to obtain a perfectly vertical line. To say something is plumb is to say it is perpendicular, absolute and true. In a crooked world, aren't you glad He's left us the straight way? His Word is our moral plumb line in a world of no morality. His Word is our truth plumb line in a culture that claims there is no truth. His Word is our guide when we don't know where to go. In His Word we learn about the Father's heart toward us. Mary knew that listening to Jesus would be a crucial step on her Avenue to Desire. It was the one thing that was needed. She loved Him passionately because she knew Him. And she knew Him because she spent time listening to His Word. We will never love someone or trust someone we do not know.

- *Muse on Psalm 27:4. "One thing I ask of the
  LORD, this is what I seek: that I may dwell in the
  house of the LORD all the days of my life, to gaze
  upon the beauty of the LORD and to seek him in his
  temple."*

Third stop on the Avenue to Desire is a Priority Check-up. Are
we spending time, like Mary, at Jesus' feet? Perhaps this is the
first time you've even heard of such a concept. Or maybe you've
heard it's important to spend time with the Lord but are clueless
about how to begin. Not to worry. There are some simple ways to
get started. Read the Gospel of John and then through the rest
of the New Testament. Pray before you begin, asking the Lord
to help you understand what you are reading. Using a journal
can be a good way to track your journey with the Lord. Write
down what you are learning, questions you have, and even prayer
requests. You can also read the Bible in a year. It takes about 15
minutes a day. Or even read a few Psalms a day and pray about
what you learn. Maybe join a Bible study where you can learn
with other people about the Lord. The point is, start. Do it daily
and watch your love for the Lord explode.

HER PLACE

Mary of Bethany, more than anyone else, is associated with the
feet of Jesus. Every time we run into her, we find her prostrate. In
times of joy she anointed His feet with sweet perfume. In times
of grief she fell at His feet and wept. In times of criticism she sat
at His feet and listened. What a stunning picture of humility,
dependence, surrender and a profound model for us. Where do
you go in your seasons of joy? Your times of grief and despair?
Your times when critics abound? We must go to Him just as
humble and as needy as Mary. How is that done? For me, it's
through prayer. I pour out my heart to Him no matter how I

feel. I spend a great deal of time in the Psalms. There I learn that no emotion is sinful but that God uses them all to draw us to Himself. Listen to what Psalm 142:1-3 has to say:

> I cry aloud to the LORD; I lift up my voice to the LORD for mercy. I pour out my complaint before him; before him I tell my trouble.
>
> When my spirit grows faint within me, it is you who know my way.

King David was in a cave hiding from his enemies when he wrote this. He was sad, lonely and scared. Do you see how he just told the Lord what he was feeling? So can we. We can cry, beg for mercy, voice our complaints and confess our abject exhaustion. We'll delve more fully into the key role prayer plays on our Avenue to Intimacy in the final chapter of this book. But suffice it to say that finding our place at the feet of Jesus is greatly enhanced when we pray. Pray often, pray through the Psalms, and pray about everything.

From Mary's life we've seen that the Avenue to Desire is open to all who are willing to grow in their love and commitment to Christ and keep Him as a priority in their lives. Sure, we will falter along the way, but let the memories of His love woo you back.

- *Let Zephaniah 3:17 reverberate around your soul. "The LORD your God is with you, he is mighty to save. He will take great delight in you, he will quiet you with his love, he will rejoice over you with singing."*

Meditations for the Journey
DESIRE

Consider . . .

God's Word

I am always with you; you hold me by my right hand. You guide me with your counsel, and afterward you will take me into glory. Whom have I in heaven but you? And earth has nothing I desire besides you. My flesh and my heart may fail, but God is the strength of my heart and my portion forever.

Psalm 73:23-26

God's Heart

O God, quicken to life every power within me, that I may lay hold of eternal things. Open my eyes that I may see; give me acute spiritual perception; enable me to taste Thee and know that Thou art good. Make heaven more real to me than any earthly thing has ever been. Amen.

A.W. Tozer, *The Pursuit of God*

*Meditations
for the Journey
Desire*

Following Him

*When I Can't See
the End of the Road*

52

 *Singing* . . .

Take My Life and Let It Be

*Take my life and let it be consecrated, Lord, to
Thee; take my hands and let them move at the
impulse of Thy love.*

*Take my feet and let them be swift and
beautiful for Thee; take my voice and let me
sing always, only, for my King.*

*Take my lips and let them be filled with
messages for Thee; take my silver and my
gold—not a mite would I withhold.*

*Take my love—my God, I pour at Thy feet its
treasure store; take myself—and I will be ever,
only, all for Thee.*

Frances R. Havergal, 1836-1879

 *Praying* . . .

*Precious heavenly Father, I surrender all my
life to You . . . again. I hope that's OK. I seem
to keep taking it back . . . but I really want to
present it to You as my spiritual act of worship.
You are my desire. I **seek** only You. Be pleased
with my offering of myself.*

> *"My coming to faith did not start with a leap but rather a series of staggers from what seemed like one safe place to another."*
>
> **Anne Lamott**
> *Traveling Mercies*

Avenue to FREEDOM

Some years ago, Bob and I visited Russia while it was still part of the Soviet Union. To get there we had to go through the infamous border guards protecting the Motherland from unwanted outside influence. It was an encounter I will never forget. Young soldiers were seated in large, glass-encased guard posts. The whole arrangement set the stage for intimidation. One by one, passengers were motioned to move forward toward the checkpoint. The guards wanted to see our passports and visas and then, with a scowl, they would stare at us for what seemed like an eternity! They'd look at our passports and then at us, our passports and us. It was frightening. I didn't know if I should cry, scream or get back on the airplane and head for home. Meanwhile, other groups of soldiers rifled through our suitcases, opening up every container, unfolding each piece of clothing. The whole unsettling process took over an hour. Our trip had only begun, and I was already sorely aware of a privilege I had taken for granted daily in the United States of America. *Freedom.* Freedom allows creativity, ingenuity and growth. The lack of it leaves people hopeless, unable to dream and stripped of real life. At the core, all people long for freedom.

54

* *Ponder how important freedom is to you.*

* *Has there been a time in your life when your freedom was taken away?*

Just because Americans enjoy political freedom, that doesn't guarantee freedom for the soul. Spiritual freedom begins when we become a follower of Christ, allow the Holy Spirit to lead and guide us each day, and then choose to stay clear of the passing pleasures of sin which can so easily entangle us. (Hebrews 11:25). The Avenue to Freedom is a key part of our journey toward intimacy with the Father. God created us to be His. He designed us to be free. He gave us a heart where He was to be installed as King. But things went tragically awry. A.W. Tozer captures it well:

> Before the Lord God made man upon the earth He first prepared for him by creating a world of useful and pleasant things for his sustenance and delight. In the Genesis account of the creation these are called simply "things." They were made for man's uses, but they were meant always to be external to the man and subservient to him. In the deep heart of the man was a shrine where none but God was worthy to come. Within him was God; without, a thousand gifts, which God had showered upon him.

> But sin has introduced complications and has made those very gifts of God a potential source of ruin to the soul. Our woes began when God was forced out of His central shrine and "things" were allowed to enter. Within the human heart "things" have taken over. Men have now by nature no peace within their hearts, for God is crowned there no longer, but there in the moral dusk stubborn and aggressive usurpers fight among themselves for first place on the throne. (*The Pursuit of God*)

- *Who or what is on the throne of your life?*

- *Identify some aggressive usurpers.*

As believers we must remain vigilant in our struggle against the subtle and not-so-subtle usurpers who would vie for control. We must ask God for strength to stand strong. I see these characteristics in a woman whose story is recorded in all four Gospels. She's not a standout or a main player. If fact, you'd miss her if you were not looking for her. The Avenue to Freedom was marked with plenty of pits, pinnacles and pivotal points, but she thrived and left behind extraordinary lessons.

When we first meet Mary Magdalene, she wasn't following the Lord, but was desperate for change. Jesus didn't find her in a pretty place, but in a place of pitiful bondage. That's good news for those who are reading this book and find themselves in a messy spot. People in such a position often feel they are so far away from God that He couldn't find them, even if He tried. Many know what it's like to be captured by drugs, drink, sex, shopping, gambling, anger or any of a whole host of modern-day enemies that impound the soul. For Mary Magdalene, things were about to take an abrupt about-face. She was to meet the bondage-breaker and experience a level of freedom she never dreamed possible.

- *Identify the issues that impound your soul.*

SET FREE

Even before Jesus saw Mary Magdalene, He'd announced His intention to bring freedom. During a hometown synagogue service early in His ministry He said, "The Spirit of the Lord is on me, because he has anointed me to preach good news to the poor. He has sent me to proclaim freedom for the prisoners and recovery of sight for the blind, to release the oppressed, to proclaim the year of the Lord's favor" (Luke 4:18-19). Many places in the Old Testament tell of God's heart for His people to be free. "The Lord looked down from his sanctuary on high, from heaven he viewed the earth, to hear the groans of the prisoners and release those condemned to death" (Psalm 102:19-20). The freedom Jesus was offering was not a free pass out of a literal jail, but a radical invitation to spiritual freedom. Jesus said, "I am the light of the world. Whoever follows me will never walk in darkness" (John 8:12).

• *List any areas of darkness in your life.*

Wherever Jesus went He brought deliverance to all who would believe. He still does that today, and becoming a Christian is the first step on the Avenue to Freedom. When we ask Christ to come into our lives, a marvelous transformation takes place in our spiritual life. We are delivered from the kingdom of darkness and given entrance into the kingdom of light (Colossians 1:12-14). Aren't you glad? I would have crashed and burned years ago had the Lord not opened my eyes to see and experience His love and forgiveness, a new reason and resource for living.

Jesus came to bring freedom. It was a major component in His mission. But He came to bring that freedom to individuals with a name, a face and a story. This encounter with Mary Magdalene in Luke 8:1-3, is a graphic example of an individual accepting the freedom Christ offered and walking in newness of life.

> After this, Jesus traveled about from one town and
> village to another, proclaiming the good news of the
> kingdom of God. The Twelve were with him, and also
> some women who had been cured of evil sprits and

diseases: Mary (called Magdalene) from whom seven
demons had come out; Joanna the wife of Cuza, the
manager of Herod's household; Susanna; and many
others. These women were helping to support them out
of their own means.

Let's explore the few details given to us in the book of Luke.
First, Mary lived in the town of Magdala, on the west coast
of the Sea of Galilee, about two miles south of Capernaum.
Historians tell us that Magdala was a thriving and populous
place. Dry works and textile factories made it a prosperous
community. Some have suggested that Mary was wealthy because
she supported Jesus from her own means. Secondly, it is most
likely that she was single and without family obligations. We will
discover, as our study of her continues, that she followed Jesus
from Galilee to Jerusalem. Jesus broke time-honored traditions
that kept women at arms-length from the things of God. For
example, there was a court for women in the temple, but only
men proceeded beyond that point. Not so with Jesus. He always
welcomed women to come close and, in so doing, set in motion a
freedom for women that blesses us still.

- **_Thank Him for welcoming you._**

Finally, we learn from this passage that evil spirits troubled Mary.
Exactly how they affected her, we do not know; but we do know
that once she was set free, she was released into the beauty of
a life devoted to the Lord. That is the nature of freedom. It's
not just escaping from past troubles, but also moving toward
something that deeply satisfies. When we meet Mary, she is a
new woman, counted among Jesus' closest friends, part of the
band of disciples, and taking the good news of the Gospel to
others still desperate for change.

The Avenue to Freedom takes us from a place of hurt to healing, and from bondage to release. Jesus came to set us free and to give us life abundantly (Galatians 5:1 and John 10:10).

- *Confess those things that prevent you from experiencing His life of freedom.*

The Lord did for Mary what she could never do for herself. He set her free. She was stuck and the Lord came to her rescue. Most of us can relate to the feeling of being stuck, bound with no hope of escape because a habit or lifestyle choice has taken over. But Jesus' same life-changing power is still available to us today no matter what has enveloped our lives. First John 2:15-16 gives great insight into the things that ensnare us:

> Do not love the world or anything in the world. If anyone loves the world, the love of the Father is not in him. For everything in the world—the cravings of sinful man, the lust of his eyes and the boasting of what he has and does—comes not from the Father, but from the world.

The "world" John refers to isn't the physical realm that God created in all its beauty and splendor, but rather "a system of values and goals from which God is excluded" (Walvoord and Zuck, *The Bible Knowledge Commentary*). The cravings of sinful man, the lust of his eyes, and the boasting of what he has and does are phrases that John uses to describe the world's system.

The natural cravings of humanity are probably best understood as a preoccupation with gratifying our God-given physical desires. They come in all shapes and sizes: food, sex, and relaxation, just to name a few. In our time the preoccupation with sex is a dominant feature. It's everywhere—television, movies, music, billboards and on the cover of virtually every magazine. Some turn to Internet pornography, "gentlemen's clubs," prostitution or

affairs. Many marriages and individual lives have been invaded
and devastated by these practices. For others, romance novels,
soap operas and inappropriate Internet chat rooms have become
places where the frustrated can vicariously live out their fantasies.
It seems safe but always leads to deeper levels of involvement and
bondage, ultimately taking over our lives.

Wanting something we do not possess is what the Bible calls
coveting or the lust of the eyes. Coveting is not only self-
destructive but leads to hurtful decisions against others as well
as ourselves. At the root lies a general dissatisfaction with one's
lot in life, leading to comparison, jealousy and envy. If you have
ever experienced inward delight over the demise of a person who
appears to "have it all," then you have faced this common enemy
called envy. Other telltale signs include shopping too much,
spending too much, and dreaming too much about how better
life would be if we only had _____. (You fill in the blank.)
Let's face it, all of us have propensities in these areas.

Boasting of what we have and do is such a common practice in
our culture. It speaks to our tendency to be obsessed with our
own status, accomplishments and importance. We can judge
ourselves or others based on the neighborhood we live in, the cars
we drive, the "toys" we possess, the vacations we take, who we
know, what we do, the jewelry we wear . . . you get the picture.
We crave importance, and our desire to attain it can become a
driving force in our lives.

These three aspects of "the world" that are identified in 1 John 2,
are Tozer's "stubborn and aggressive usurpers that fight among
themselves for first place on the throne." This is the place where
Jesus alone must dwell in order for us to experience true freedom.

- ***Think about how the world system has affected
  you in these three areas.***

So, how about it? Are you stuck in any area of your life? Honesty is crucial if you plan to get to the other side and experience freedom. The power of Christ is the only power greater than sin (Romans 8:1-16). It's never too late. It begins by humbly acknowledging your need for God to do a fresh work in your life. Is there a dark corner of your life that you need to face? Bring it into the light. Does sin need to be confessed? Talk with the Lord about it (Proverbs 28:11). Are there relationships that need mending? Make a phone call. Do you need accountability? Find a safe friend whom you can trust. You catch my drift. It is our responsibility to face head-on the issues that keep us in bondage, and then trust the Lord for strength to change.

- *Consider what action step needs to be taken.*

- *What will stop you from action?*

Thomas Merton correctly summed up the essence of being Christian: "Simply to be people who are content to live close to him and to renew the kind of life in which closeness is felt and experienced" (as quoted in *The Ragamuffin Gospel*). Be done with all that would hinder your journey on the Avenue to Freedom.

SET AFLAME

It's hard to imagine how dramatically Mary's life must have changed. Although the details of her past remain largely unknown, the way she lived her life from the healing on is recorded in the New Testament. It is obvious this dear woman was grateful and expressed her thanks in wholehearted surrender to Jesus. The physical and mental tortures of bondage gone, she now chose to commit the rest of her life to following Him. The delivered became a disciple. Love is so becoming.

- *Meditate on Psalm 40:1-3. "I waited patiently for the LORD; he turned to me and heard my cry. He lifted me out of the slimy pit, out of the mud and mire; he set my feet on a rock and gave me a firm place to stand. He put a new song in my mouth, a hymn of praise to our God. Many will see and fear and put their trust in the LORD."*

- *Has this been true for you?*

Mary expressed her love and gratitude for the Lord in different ways. She followed Him from Galilee to Jerusalem. Matthew 27:55 (also recorded in Mark 15: 40-41 and Luke 8:3) tells us:

> Many women were there, watching from a distance. They had followed Jesus from Galilee to care for his needs. Among them were Mary Magdalene, Mary the mother of James and Joses, and the mother of Zebedee's sons.

Jesus and His disciples were constantly on the move and Mary, along with other women, helped to make the journey easier. She was a person of means, so she gave Him money. She was completely changed, so she probably joined in bringing others to Jesus to receive the same kind of help. It was the least she could do for the One who had done so much for her.

- *Name some ways you have given back to the Lord.*

She went all the way to Jerusalem with Him. She must have witnessed the worshiping crowds on Palm Sunday. She was in town during the Last Supper, Judas' betrayal, the prayer meeting in the Garden of Gethsemane, the phony trials, the cruel beatings and the criminal death on a cross. Many disciples fled. One denied. One betrayed. She stayed close to Him. In the above reference the verse begins, "Many women were there, watching from a distance." The context of that verse is the whole ordeal leading up to the death of Jesus. John 19:25 tells us that Mary Magdalene was at the cross when Jesus died. Luke 23:55 tells us that her presence did not stop there.

> The women who had come with Jesus from Galilee followed Joseph and saw the tomb and how his body was laid in it. Then they went home and prepared spices and perfumes.

Mary was fearless in her devotion to Jesus. She did not flee but continued to follow her Savior to the very end of His life and beyond.

Oh, how I want to love the Lord the way Mary did—gratefully and sacrificially. It was an open love expressed in obvious ways. That must be one of the results when we step out onto the Avenue to Freedom. The apostle Paul puts it all together for us in Ephesians 5:2:

> Live a life of love, just as Christ loved us and gave himself up for us as a fragrant offering and sacrifice to God.

Are you living a life of love toward God? What would that look like? It would have to include spending time with Him on a consistent basis by reading His Word, talking with Him about all that concerns you, practicing praise, and following even when it gets hard.

Richard Foster begins to capture the flavor of such a love in his book *Devotional Classics:*

> The divine love of God in Christ both purifies and inflames. The love of God is no sentimental slop. It burns away everything that is of a nature contrary to

itself. Nothing can abide if it stands in opposition to divine love. Also, this love comforts, draws, nurtures and inflames us with desire for the beloved. It is a 'love that will not let us go,' as the old hymn writer aptly confessed. May you and I be more and more drawn in, taken over and consumed by this love from God.

• *Pause and pray. Think about His love.*

Mary's interaction with the Lord did not end with His death. God had a surprise for this sweet disciple. Guess who would be the first to greet Him alive that early Sunday morning? Mary Magdalene.

The other disciples were nowhere to be seen. John, the beloved disciple, is recorded present in John 19 but did not appear again until after the Resurrection. Mary's heart of love planned to attend the body with spices and perfumes the next morning, in much the same way as we'd bring flowers to a gravesite today.

The sorrow of losing her beloved Savior jumps out when you read John 20:1-18. It was real, pinching and unrelenting grief. Mary returned to the tomb while it was still dark, realizing immediately that Jesus' body was not there. She found Peter and John, and told them. They ran to the tomb, and seeing that it was empty, believed her report. Peter and John went back to their homes, but Mary stayed at the gravesite, weeping. So like Mary. Then she saw the angels and heard the voice she knew so well. Jesus. He called her by name and she cried again, not for her loss but for the unbelievable find. Her Savior was before her, alive! He asked, "Why are you crying?" showing personal concern for her. He gave her new responsibilities. "Go to my brothers and tell them I am returning to my Father and your Father, my God and your God." Can you imagine the thrill and the sheer joy? The One her heart loved was before her.

• *Place yourself in Mary's position.*

• *How would you be feeling?*

• *What would you do?*

Hebrews 11:6 gives us some good insight into the faith I see in Mary: "Without faith it is impossible to please God, because anyone who comes to him must believe that he exists and that he rewards those who earnestly seek him." Mary was a seeker of the Lord, and look how she was rewarded. She was the first human being to see Him alive. She was given the command to go to the cowering disciples and tell them the news of His resurrection. An amazing honor for this unassuming woman.

This is the last time we see Mary in the New Testament, but there are a few timeless lessons that still speak loudly and clearly all these years later. We see what Christ can do for a woman. He can free her in the deepest, most needy places in her life and give her peace. Do you know the peace that passes understanding (Philippians 4:7)? Are there still areas in your life where you are compromising with sin, pretending God cannot see, or thinking it has no effect on your life (Hebrews 4:13)? Friend, it's time to get free and stay free by coming to Him, learning to be alert to Satan's schemes (Ephesians 6:10-18), taking every thought captive (2 Corinthians 10:3-5), and doing what is pleasing to the Lord (Ephesians 5:10).

Mary demonstrates what a woman can do for Christ. She practiced her faith by leaving all to follow Him. She gave her time and money and became a joyful witness of His resurrection. She loved Him in very practical, quiet ways. And we can do the same today. What a privilege it is to be able to serve the God of all glory! Jesus talked about this in John 12:26:

> Whoever serves me must follow me; and where I am, my servant also will be. My father will honor the one who serves me.

Mary was clearly honored by the Lord when He showed Himself first to her that memorable Sunday morning.

- ***Think of ways God has honored your love and obedience.***

The Avenue to Freedom begins when we come to Jesus for salvation. It continues as we find new release from the clutches of sin. Once free, our lives are set in an entirely new direction, our love for Him refreshed and invigorated, our desire to serve Him renewed. We are now able to hear how much He loves us. When we are living in rebellion we don't have ears to hear His voice.

I am deeply moved by the way Brennan Manning imagines the Lord speaking to us.

> "Has it crossed your mind that I am proud you accepted the gift of faith I offered you? Proud that you freely chose Me, after I had chosen you, as your friend and Lord? Proud that with all your warts and wrinkles you haven't given up? Proud that you believe in Me enough to try again and again? Are you aware how I appreciate you for wanting Me?" (*Reflections for Ragamuffins*)

- *Reflect on Jesus' love for you.*

- *Pray Psalm 18:1-3 back to Him. "I love you, O LORD, my strength. The LORD is my rock, my fortress and my deliverer; my God is my rock, in whom I take refuge. He is my shield and the horn of my salvation, my stronghold. I call to the LORD, who is worthy of praise, and I am saved from my enemies."*

Mary Magdalene's life points us toward the Avenue to Freedom. It may not always be easy or convenient. It will undoubtedly require surrender and sacrifice, both extremely unpopular concepts in our culture. But the results outweigh the cost because this avenue will lead us closer to the place of intimacy. Shall we make the pilgrimage together?

Meditations for the Journey
FREEDOM

Consider . . .

God's Word

*I run in the path of your commands, for you
have set my heart free.*

Psalm 119:32

*I will walk about in freedom, for I have sought
out your precepts.*

Psalm 119:45

God's Heart

*Stop trying to be perfect in order to deserve My
love. You will never be "enough" of anything,
anyway. I do not want your worth, your
efforts, your gifts and credentials and produce.
I want you simply because you are you. If
tomorrow you should become anything other
than what you are today, still I would want
you. If you were in a horrible fire and burned
beyond recognition, if you contracted a dread
disease and became deaf and dumb, if you
could not lift a finger to love anymore, still I
would want you. My love is for you, and not
for what you are.*

Ruth Senter, *Longing for Love*

*Meditations
for the Journey
Freedom*

Following Him

*When I Can't See
the End of the Road*

68

'Tis So Sweet to Trust in Jesus

*'Tis so sweet to trust in Jesus, just to take Him
at His word, just to rest upon His promise, just
to know, "Thus saith the Lord."*

*O how sweet to trust in Jesus, just to trust His
cleansing blood, just in simple faith to plunge
me 'neath the healing, cleansing flood.*

*Yes, 'tis sweet to trust in Jesus, just from sin
and self to cease, just from Jesus simply taking
life and rest and joy and peace.*

*I'm so glad I learned to trust Thee, precious
Jesus, Savior, Friend; and I know that Thou
art with me, wilt be with me to the end.*

*Chorus: Jesus, Jesus, how I trust Him! How
I've proved Him o'er and o'er! Jesus, Jesus,
precious Jesus! O for grace to trust Him more!*

Louisa M. Stead, 1850-1917

*O Lord Jesus, You came to set me free! Thank
You for freeing me from my sin and shame,
from my guilty conscience and the grasp of
Satan. And now I choose to follow You all the
days of my life. My food is to do Your will and
to bring You pleasure. I want my life to make
You smile.* **Amen.**

> *"Love unexpressed grows cold, and soon*
> *it is not love at all but an arrangement."*
>
> **Sylvia Gunter,**
> *Prayer Essentials for Living in His Presence, Vol. 1*

Avenue to LOVE

I have some very specific memories of love—those times when I knew that I was cherished. My sixth birthday was one of them. I had a big swim party with cake, balloons and a clown. By the time everyone left, I figured the festivities had ended. I walked through our living room and there it was. Sitting on the patio was a blue, fully-loaded Schwinn bike. It had baskets on the front and the back and very cool streamers attached to the ends of the handle bars. The first words out of my mouth were, "Mom and Dad, someone left their bike here." That's when they shouted, "Happy Birthday! It's your new bike." At that moment, I felt completely loved.

Years later, during my junior year in high school, a different expression of love touched my heart. It was an ordinary day. School, track practice and then to work at the local mall. When I returned home, I found a poem on my desk that my mother had written for me. There was no special occasion, just an

opportunity she had taken to remind me of her love. It's framed
and in my office today. She titled it, "At Seventeen:"

Think of fluid golden honey,
Think of warmth,
Think of softly smiling eyes,
Think of arms around you,
Think of love. That's Barbara.

Think of grace and style,
Think of liquid movement,
Think of lightness,
Think of gaiety and laughter,
Think of love. That's Barbara.

Think ripeness,
Think of fullness and fulfilling,
Think of promise,
Think of giving,
Think of love. That's Barbara.

Think of strength,
Think of depths of understanding,
Think of forgiving,
Think of life,
Think of love. That's Barbara.

Know I love you,
Mother

You have memories, too. Times when you've been surprised by love, amazed that someone was thinking about you when they didn't have to and then did something to say it in ways you'd understand: "I love you."

- ***Remember a gesture of love shown to you.***

- ***Recall a time when you initiated such an act.***

For many of you, trying to dig up a few examples of being loved is quite a challenge. You may be a child brought up in a damaged family where violence and abuse were common occurrences, and may find it very hard to raise a single memory of love. And if your adult life has been troubled and disappointing, believing love is out there can be difficult at best.

- ***If pain and hurt fill your mind, pray and ask the Lord to show you His love in rich, healing ways.***

- ***Meditate on Psalm 34:18. "The LORD is close to the brokenhearted and saves those who are crushed in spirit."***

I am so thankful that the God we worship understands all the intricate details of our lives, both good and bad, and loves us anyway. Consider how King David articulated this truth in Psalm 139:1-6:

> O LORD, you have searched me and you know me. You know when I sit and when I rise; you perceive my thoughts from afar. You discern my going out and my lying down; you are familiar with all my ways. Before a word is on my tongue you know it completely, O LORD. You hem me in—behind and before; you have laid your

hand upon me. Such knowledge is too wonderful for me, too lofty for me to attain.

Coming to grips with the tender affection of God, no matter the circumstance, is what the journey down the Avenue of Love is all about. This is a constant battle for me. I think that's why He has used the women in Scripture to be observable examples of what His love looks like and what He can do in the lives of those who receive it. The biblical guide who will lead us deeper into God's heart is Mary, Jesus' mother. She was truly unique among women, called to give birth to and nurture the Son of God. We see her through each of the Gospels, over a 33-year period, stopping often to learn lessons as she experienced God's closeness at both the peaks and valleys in her life.

One unknown author has posed a few questions for Mary:

What was it like watching Him pray?

When He saw a rainbow, did He ever mention a flood?

Did you ever feel awkward teaching Him how He created the world?

When He saw a lamb being led to the slaughter, did He act differently?

Did you ever see Him with a distant look on His face as if He were listening to someone you couldn't hear?

Did the thought ever occur to you that the God to whom you were praying was asleep under your own roof?

Did you ever try to count the stars with Him . . . and succeed?

Did He ever wake up afraid?

Did you ever think, "That's God eating my soup"?

SETTING THE STAGE

Mary, the mother of Jesus, is one of the most familiar women in the Bible. Let's put her in the right historical context. She lived in Nazareth, a town situated in the southern ranges of Galilee. Nazareth did not have the best reputation. Because it was located on a major trade route, Gentile traders and Roman soldiers spent a lot of time there, bringing with them more than their wares. It was a town known for its many religions and its lack of morals.

Luke 1:26-56 is the longest account in the New Testament of Mary's early life. When the angel Gabriel appeared to her she was probably only 12 to 14 years of age. She was a virgin and engaged to be married to Joseph. Walvoord and Zuck's *Bible Knowledge Commentary* notes that "in Jewish culture then a man and woman were betrothed or pledged to each other for a period of time before the actual consummation of their marriage. This betrothal was much stronger than an engagement period today, for the two were considered husband and wife except that they did not live together till after the wedding."

When Gabriel spoke to Mary, she was alone. There is no telling exactly where in Nazareth she was or just what she was doing. But what is clear is that the angel had a very special message for her that would change her life completely.

HER HEART FOR GOD

Nothing is said in the Word about Mary's physical beauty, but much is said of her beautiful character, especially her love for God. Both the angel Gabriel and Mary's relative Elizabeth recognized this quality in her life. Gabriel's announcement to her was astounding. I cannot recall another place in the Bible where an angel speaks like this to a human: "Greetings, you who are highly favored! The Lord is with you." Mary was highly favored because God had chosen her to bear His Son. But these words were also an essential recognition of her spiritual fitness for such an honored visit and high calling. God was an integral part of her young life. Because Mary's child was to be holy and undefiled, she herself had to be pursuing a life that pleased the Lord. She had a real relationship with the God of Abraham, Isaac and Jacob, cultivated over years of spending time with Him in His Word. God came to her at that moment in an unusual way, to be sure, but she already knew Him well. That doesn't mean she was sinless. In her song of praise to God in Luke 1:47 she referred to Him as her "Savior," thus acknowledging her need for forgiveness and for salvation from her sin.

- **Consider what a life pleasing to the Lord looks like.**

After the encounter with the angel, Mary went to be with her relative Elizabeth, who was herself six months pregnant. Listen to what Elizabeth said to Mary: "Blessed is she who has *believed* that what the Lord has said to her will be accomplished!" Elizabeth was clearly applauding Mary's faith in God. Faith is built and buoyed by our love and knowledge of God.

Mary's faith stood out to Elizabeth because it contrasted with what she had seen in her own husband. Zechariah had not believed when the same angel had appeared to him six months earlier. Luke 1:5-25 tells the story. Elizabeth and Zechariah were godly people, "well along in years," and had no children. He was a priest and had been chosen that day to go into the Holy Place to burn incense. While he was in the temple, Gabriel appeared to him with the good news: "Do not be afraid, Zechariah; your prayer has been heard. Your wife Elizabeth will bear you a son, and you are to give him the name John." But Zechariah wanted evidence before he believed and asked Gabriel, "How can I be sure of this? I am an old man and my wife is well along in years." There were two consequences for his doubt. First, he was unable to speak until after John was born. Secondly, he received a rebuke from Gabriel for his unbelief. So it's not surprising that Elizabeth would notice the stark contrast between Zechariah's and Mary's responses.

Mary was a young girl, poor and probably uneducated, yet she trusted God with an event that would change her whole life. Zechariah, a priest well-versed in the Old Testament writings, failed this test of belief. But we see a very different priest after his son John is born. Zechariah's song of praise tells us he went much deeper with God during those nine months of silence (Luke 1:57-79).

- ***Think of a time when you struggled to trust God.***

- ***Remember an occasion when you did believe Him.***

The final example from Mary's early life in which we see her heart for God is her song of praise known as "The Magnificat." It is filled with Old Testament quotes and promises. She is humble and quick to give all glory to God for the privilege of bearing the Son of God. This song also gives us a glimpse into her deep relationship with God. It is truly amazing how well she knew the Old Testament Scriptures and how intimately she knew the Lord.

I want to continue down the Avenue to Love, and I hope you'll join me. From Mary's young life we learn of the need to develop a deep faith in God and His Word so we can be ready to respond when He asks us to obey. But how do we do that? Developing faith seems so ethereal. Romans 10:17 gives us some practical insight: "Consequently, faith comes from hearing the message, and the message is heard through the word of Christ." Faith is developed as we spend time in God's Word. Henri Nouwen challenges us on this point:

> Five or ten minutes a day may be all we can tolerate. Perhaps we are ready for an hour every day, an afternoon every week, a day every month, or a week every year. The amount of time will vary for each person according to temperament, age, job, lifestyle, and maturity. But we do not take the spiritual life seriously if we do not set aside some time to be with God and listen to Him. We may have to write it in black and white in our daily calendar so that nobody else can take away this period of time. Then we will be able to say to our friends, neighbors, students, customers, clients, or patients, "I am sorry, but I've already made an appointment at that time and it can't be changed."

- *How has your faith been strengthened by time in the Word?*

- *Decide if changes need to be made.*

- *Read though Psalm 19:7-11.*

HER SUBMISSION TO GOD

Mary's love for God was more than an emotion; it was a commitment to obey. Perhaps the most amazing aspect of Gabriel's announcement is the way Mary received it willingly and submissively. She spoke only twice during the encounter. First, like Zechariah, she asked a question, but it was one founded in curiosity, not doubt. She was a virgin and didn't quite understand how this whole process was to take place. Gabriel assured her that it would be a miraculous conception orchestrated by the Holy Spirit. The next time we hear her voice is when she simply says, "I am the Lord's servant . . . May it be to me as you have said." What innocent acceptance!

I would have had a few more questions: What about Joe? Who's going to tell him? What about my parents? Will Gabriel tell them this is a miracle and not immorality? I certainly would have wanted a little time to pray about the whole proposal. Maybe this angel could come back tomorrow.

No such response came from Mary's lips, even though her reputation could be smeared. God's will for her life was clear and she said "yes." There were no conditions for her submission. She loved and trusted God, so she obeyed. God would take care of all the important details. An angel did appear to Joseph and told him to take Mary as his wife because the Holy Spirit conceived the child in her womb. Joseph did as he was commanded, married Mary, had no physical union with her until after the child was born, and named the child Jesus (Matthew 1:18-25).

I need her example because I do have parameters around my obedience. I am so prone to do what pleases me and enhances my comfort. The whole idea of complete submission to *anything* that He may ask seems scary. Frankly, I'd rather have it my way, like visiting a good salad bar. The experience allows me the freedom to build my plate any way I choose. I once read an article on how the restaurants arrange the items. The strategy is to place all the inexpensive selections at the beginning of the bar and the expensive ones at the end. Now that I am an educated patron, I adjust my approach. I begin at the end of the bar, placing nuts and meats on the bottom. I like fruit in a salad, so next come raisins and pineapple, skipping the onions, and then I add lots of mushrooms and beets. I may skip the lettuce altogether! When I finish, it is a perfect creation. Others may do it differently; that's their choice. But I don't care. It's my salad, not theirs, and I will fix it the way I want to.

This may be a delightful way to make a salad, but it's an erroneous way to live the Christian life. Yet that's exactly what I've been guilty of doing. God has shown me that I do not have the right to pick and choose what I want to obey and what I don't. When I became a Christian I was so thankful that forgiveness was part of the deal (Ephesians 1:7)! That's an item I'd put on the plate. I was also thrilled that the Bible spoke of a loving God who'd never leave me (Hebrews 13:5). Another selection I want to heap on my plate. But there were *other* commands like "Love your enemies" (Matthew 5:44) or "do everything without complaining or arguing" (Phillipians 2:14) which I found less appealing. The Lord has reminded me of what He says in John 14:21: "Whoever has my commands and obeys them, he is the one who loves me. He who loves me will be loved by my Father, and I too will love him and show myself to him." Obedience is a by-product of love. If I struggle with obedience, I don't need more rules. I need to fall in love. Intimacy and submission go hand in hand. The more I know the Lord, and the more I love Him, the more inclined I am to follow His commands . . . even when it's costly. Mary knew this was the only way to proceed down the Avenue to Love. Oswald Chambers, in his classic devotional work *My Utmost for His Highest*, writes:

> My personal life may be crowded with small petty incidents, altogether unnoticeable and mean; but if I obey Jesus Christ in the haphazard circumstances, they become pinholes through which I see the face of God, and when I stand face to face with God I will discover that through my obedience thousands were blessed.

It was true for Mary and it will be true for us as we choose to surrender our wills to His.

- *Determine if you have a "salad bar" mentality to obeying the Lord.*

- *If changes are needed, ask Him for help. Read Psalm 51.*

- *Ponder Jesus' words in the Garden of Gethsemane: "Father, if you are willing, take this cup from me; yet not my will, but yours be done" (Luke 22:42).*

HER HEART TO SERVE

The qualities of Mary's life are blended together to form a picture of the whole person. She knew God and was willing to do whatever He said. God wanted Mary to be Jesus' mother. The Spirit conceived Jesus but He grew in her womb, was delivered through her body, nursed at her breast, and grew up in her home. Mary influenced her Son to be a diligent lover of God and an ardent follower of His Word, just as she was. I wonder if Deuteronomy 6:4-7 was on her mind?

Hear, O Israel: The LORD our God, the LORD is one.
Love the LORD your God with all your heart and
with all your soul and with all your strength. These
commandments that I give you today are to be upon
your hearts. Impress them on your children. Talk about
them when you sit at home and when you walk along
the road, when you lie down and when you get up.

Jesus grew up with a desire to please His Father. "The world must
learn that I love the Father and that I do exactly what my Father
has commanded me" (John 14:31). Mary served the Lord in the
area He asked her to and must have had great satisfaction as she
watched her Son grow.

The question each of us must ask is: Are we doing what the Lord
wants us to do? Whether it is in the home, the office, on the
jobsite or in the operating room, we must "work at it with all
your heart, as working for the Lord . . . It is the Lord Christ you
are serving" (Colossians 3:23-24).

- *How has God called you to serve Him?*

- *Are there any areas where you are resisting Him?*

HER HEART TO SUFFER

Mary's deep faith, complete submission, and willingness to
serve the Lord in the way He asked are helpful markers for us
on the Avenue to Love. If we want to continue to pursue greater
intimacy with God, these same qualities need to be growing
in our lives. There is another aspect of Mary's life we need to
consider. For the majority of her life she experienced a great deal
of suffering. She knew both delight and darkness on her Avenue
to Love. The precious, God-given baby who brought so much joy

would not stay in the manger. He would become a man, begin His ministry, and experience rejection leading to His death on the cross. He would be her Son and her Savior, and the journey would not be easy.

Suffering was predicted early on in Mary's life by Simeon in Luke 2:35. Mary and Joseph were required by Jewish law to present their firstborn Son to God 33 days after His birth. Simeon, a godly older man, was in the temple courts that very day. God had promised him that he would see the Messiah before he died. When Joseph and Mary brought Jesus to the temple, Simeon held the Savior in his arms and praised God (Luke 2: 29-32). His next words were directed toward Mary: "This child is destined to cause the falling and rising of many in Israel, and to be a sign that will be spoken against, so that the thoughts of many hearts will be revealed. *And a sword will pierce your own soul too*" (Luke 2:34-35, italics added).

Mary would see many come to faith in her Son and many turn away. In the process, her heart would be pierced. Let's not forget how young she was when she heard these ominous words . . . 12 to 14 years old. I wonder what went through her mind when this old man spoke to her? Perhaps Psalm 71:5 brought her comfort: "You have been my hope, O Sovereign LORD, my confidence since my youth."

There were at least four piercing wounds Mary would have to endure:

THE WOUND OF OTHERS' SUFFERING

King Herod, political king of the Jews, ordered all the boys in Bethlehem two years old and younger to be killed in a jealous attempt to kill Jesus, the newborn, true King of the Jews. God told Joseph in a dream to leave Bethlehem immediately and head for Egypt. As Mary held her Son safely in her arms she knew other mothers would watch their sons be slaughtered before their eyes—all because of her Son's mission. What sorrow and even guilt must have surrounded her during that long journey to Egypt (Matthew 2:1-17).

THE WOUND OF CHANGING RELATIONSHIPS

The first miracle of Jesus' ministry took place at a wedding in Cana of Galilee. It should have been a happy occasion. Weddings usually are. But this one held some surprises for Mary. Jesus, now about 30 years old, and His disciples had been invited to the celebration. Just as things were getting started, the wine ran out. In the Jewish culture of that time, this would have been a terrible embarrassment to the host. Jesus' mother turned to Him and said, "They have no more wine," expecting that He would remedy the situation. He turned to her and answered, "Dear woman, why do you involve me? My time has not yet come." He was not being unkind or disrespectful to his mother, just declaring His commitment to God's will and timing and not to her request. It's clear she understood exactly what He meant when she responded to the servants, "Do whatever he tells you" (John 2:1-5). This was undoubtedly a painful lesson to Mary as she watched their relationship change. She had been used to His being obedient to her (Luke 2:51), and now she must subject herself to Him.

THE WOUND OF SHARED REJECTION

It's natural for mothers to want to see their children respected and accepted. Mary had to come to grips with the divisive nature of Jesus' message. Some would love Him, but many would hate Him and seek to kill Him. Jesus was laughed at (Mark 5:40) and even accused of being demon-possessed (Luke 11:15). It must have been very difficult to hear. The hometown crowd in Nazareth was furious when they heard the Lord preach in the synagogue there (Luke 4:16-30). They even tried to throw Him off the cliff outside of town. And to make matters worse, even Mary's other sons did not believe in Him (John 7:5). At one point, His family even thought, "He is out of his mind" (Mark 3:21). It's hard to overstate the degree of pain this must have caused Mary.

THE ULTIMATE WOUND

All the other wounds paled in comparison to this final one. Mary was one of the women who stood at the foot of the cross and watched Jesus, her own dear Son, die a heinous death (John 19:25). She shared His sorrow and suffering. Can you imagine the sadness and loss of the event? There Mary's pain found its climax. Simeon's words prophesied 33 years earlier echoed in her heart. Before Jesus died He recognized His responsibility for His mother, telling John the disciple He loved to take her as his own mother. From the cross He said to Mary, "Dear woman, here is your son," and to the disciple, "Here is your mother" (John 19:26-27).

Mary experienced such great sorrow as the mother of Jesus. Even though she clearly loved God, submitted to His Word and served Him all her life, she still suffered. There is no record of her complaining or arguing with the Lord. What she said to Gabriel, "I am the Lord's servant . . . May it be to me as you have said," still held true to the end (Luke 1:38). Her uncommon love stayed strong no matter how hard things became. Why? She knew the God who planned it all. She had trusted Him when things were good and she'd continue to do so when things looked bleak. I need to be reminded of that from Mary's life. Suffering and hard times can make me fold like a cheap tent. I want to learn to see God *in* the difficulties, believe that all things work together for good for those who love Him, and come through on the other side with a more vibrant faith. Trials can do that, you know. They are God's instruments to deepen our faith. During such times of trouble we must learn to go to Him with all our feelings, fears and worries. Invite Him into the difficulty by saying, "Lord, this (name the issue at hand) is so scary for me. Please help me to keep my eyes on You. I am so prone to wander and worry when things go badly. I want to be different in this trial. Your Word says in 1 Corinthians 10:13, 'God is faithful; he will not let you be tempted beyond what you can bear. But when you are tempted, he will also provide a way out so that you can stand up under it.' Show me the way through this."

- *Evaluate your response when suffering hits.*

- *Remember a time when God encouraged you during a dark period.*

- *Pray through Psalm 31:7. "I will be glad and rejoice in your love, for you saw my affliction and knew the anguish of my soul."*

A LAST LOOK

Our last glimpse of Mary is an encouraging one. We find her on her knees in Acts 1:14, praying along with her sons and the other disciples, who now believe, waiting for the Holy Spirit. She knows the grave could not hold Jesus, that He has bodily returned to heaven, and that she will see Him again. How her sorrow must have turned to joy!

As you follow the journey of Mary's life, you see what is

needed to travel all the way on the Avenue to Love. It requires
a heart that seeks God first, submits to His will, serves Him
wholeheartedly, and is willing to do so through hard and heavy
times. Look at the biblical and post-biblical people you admire
and seek to emulate. My guess is that most of them have "Mary"
qualities in their lives.

What God did in Mary's life He wants to do in yours and mine.
Imagine that! Oh sure, the details of our stories will vary. But
what keeps me going and encouraged in my journey is knowing
that He is not finished with me yet. That's why we follow Him,
even when we can't see the end of the road. Philippians 1:6 says,
"Being confident of this, that he who began a good work in you
will carry it on to completion until the day of Christ Jesus." He
is committed to helping me grow up in Jesus and He won't give
up on me. He has promised He won't give up on you either.

I like how A.W. Tozer puts it in *The Pursuit of God:*

> He has no favorites within His household. All He has
> ever done for any of His children He will do for all of His
> children. The difference lies not with God but with us.

He has no favorites because we are all precious in His sight and
all children in His household. It's a growing confidence in this
truth that keeps us on the Avenue to Love. Someday we shall see
His face, behold His splendor and glory, and fall down before
His throne to worship Him who lives forever and ever. Believe
me, we will be so glad that we persevered.

- *Pause and pray. Clarify your commitment to
  allowing God to be God in your life.*

- *Make a mental note of what you think that would
  look like.*

- *Muse on Deuteronomy 30:19-20. "This day I call heaven and earth as witnesses against you that I have set before you life and death, blessings and curses. Now choose life, so that you and your children may live and that you may love the LORD your God, listen to his voice, and hold fast to him. For the LORD is your life . . . "*

Meditations for the Journey
LOVE

Consider...

God's Word

> ... And I pray that you, being rooted and
> established in love, may have power, together with
> all the saints, to grasp how wide and long and
> high and deep is the love of Christ, and to know
> this love that surpasses knowledge—that you may
> be filled to the measure of all the fullness of God.
> **Ephesians 3:17-19**

> And so we know and rely on the love God has for us.
> **1 John 4:16**

God's Heart

> I am here for you, child. I have always been
> here for you; I will always be here for you. You
> are My pleasure. Feel My arm around you?
> My hand in yours? I have not withdrawn My
> embrace. I hold you tightly. I go where you
> go. In fact, you cannot go anywhere that I am
> not—pigpens, ash heaps, desert shelves. I walk
> beside you—not before, not behind, but next
> to you, like good friends do. I hang on to you.
> **Ruth Senter, *Longing for Love***

*Meditations
for the Journey
Love*

Following Him

*When I Can't See
the End of the Road*

88

 *Singing* . . .

The Love of God

*The love of God is greater far than tongue or
       pen can ever tell;
It goes beyond the highest star and reaches to the lowest hell.
The guilty pair, bowed down with care,
God gave His Son to win;
His erring child He reconciled and pardoned from his sin.*

*Could we with ink the ocean fill and were the
       skies of parchment made,
Were ev'ry stalk on earth a quill and ev'ry man
       a scribe by trade,
To write the love of God above would drain the ocean dry,
Nor could the scroll contain the whole though
       stretched from sky to sky.*

*Chorus: O love of God, how rich and pure! How
       measureless and strong! It shall forevermore endure—
       the saints' and angels' song.*

Frederick M. Lehman, 1868-1953

 *Praying* . . .

*I can never fully understand Your unconditional love for
me, but I will surrender to it and accept it as true. Your
love has transformed me and reshaped my character. I have
never known a love like this. Forgive me when I doubt
Your affection and question Your care. Help me to love the
hard-to-love people in my life with the kind of love I have
received from You.* **Amen.**

> *"Prayer is the occupation of the soul with its needs.*
> *Praise is the occupation of the soul with its blessings.*
> *Worship is the occupation of the soul with God Himself."*

Alfred P. Gibbs,
Source Unknown

Avenue to WORSHIP

On Easter morning 1799, the Austrian citizens of Feldkirch awoke to find their peaceful village besieged by the army of Napoleon. Knowing that the town's defenses could not withstand an attack, those in authority hastily called a meeting to decide if they should hoist the white flag in surrender to the enemy.

The dean of the church rose first and addressed the somber assembly. "This is Easter Day," he said in a trembling voice. "This is the day of our King's Resurrection. We must have one moment of triumph. Let us at least ring the bells. If the town falls, it falls; but we must ring all the bells of Easter."

His counsel prevailed, and soon, from the church towers, the bells rang out their joyous sound; the vibrant music reverberated through the valleys and hills of Feldkirch, filling the frosty air with gladness.

The invaders, massed outside the gate, were confounded. Why should there be such a celebration? Concluding that the Austrian army had arrived during the night to relieve the town, the French

90

broke camp and were in full retreat before the bells stopped
ringing. (As quoted in *Songs of Heaven* by Robert E. Coleman)

The townsfolk must have been amazed as they watched
Napoleon's mighty army leave in retreat! They probably rang
those bells for the rest of the day. I imagine they learned quite
a significant lesson on praise and worship that was passed on
for generations. It's a lesson we need to learn as well. Praise and
worship are powerful because they call down the presence of God
into our lives and circumstances.

Worship is not limited to Sunday morning and buildings
with stained glass windows; it is to be a part of our everyday
experience with God. What does it mean to worship God? In
worship we call to mind all the attributes of God revealed in the
Bible—qualities like His patience, compassion, forgiveness and
goodness. We take time to marvel that He calls Himself our
friend, our husband, our guide and our help in times of trouble.
Worship means we put God as the number-one priority of our
life, and place everything else subservient to Him. As we make
our way down the Avenue to Worship, we will sense an increased
desire to learn how to honor Him with our life and lips.

I like how Sylvia Gunter expresses it:

> God is seeking worshipers. He desires His people to be
> eager to know Him intimately and experience all of who
> He is. He wants a people who are not content to be just
> born-again and sitting on their eternal security. He longs
> for His people not only to love Him but to be in love
> with Him. There is a difference. When you are in love,
> you desire to please your beloved more than anything
> else. You are joyfully, willingly submissive to the one
> you love. This is a commitment. This is surrender. God

would rather have you than the things you can do for
Him. He is more interested in your being all He wants
you to be than in your doing things for Him.
(*Prayer Essentials for Living in His Presence,* Vol. 1)

- *Pause and quietly tell the Lord how much you love Him.*

- *Recommit to being His and His alone.*

This is all fine and dandy when I am rested, healthy, wealthy
and wise, but what about my *real life* when I'm sick and tired,
broke and not very clever? How does God fit into the mess?
Is it possible to worship when we have a bruised heart, broken
friendships and blatant failures? The answer, my friend, is yes.
God takes our messes and graces us with His presence, His
answers and His power when we are willing to submit to Him
and wait for His timing. Everything may not be "fixed" the
way we want, but we come through the other side with stronger
character and a deeper faith. The pavement is not always smooth
when we walk down the Avenue to Worship, but we never walk
alone. Our God is there and "will take hold of your hand"
(Isaiah 42:6) and will be sure that you make it safely to the end
of the road.

- *Identify your messes.*

- *Ask the Lord to give you fresh faith.*

- *Meditate on Romans 8:28. "And we know that in all things God works for the good of those who love him, who have been called according to his purpose."*

The beauty of a woman who worshiped God despite her circumstances is seen in the life of Anna. She was a New Testament woman who learned early on that life could take some hurtful, unexpected turns. It was in these very circumstances that Anna learned to worship God. The short account of her life is found in the gospel of Luke. There are three verses in the Bible about her, only 81 words. But from this synopsis we glean nuggets of gold so precious we must linger over her life and use it as a model for our own. We are going to look at how God developed her life and how she then devoted her life to Him so she'd be ready, willing and able to declare to others that the Savior had come. Each of these markers on the Avenue to Worship will give us important instruction on the ingredients of a worshipful life.

HER LIFE DEVELOPED

Learning to worship God doesn't just happen because we go to church, sing inspiring hymns or choruses, know the Christian lingo and attend a few conferences. It happens as we choose to submit to the developmental process God ordains. We make daily choices to believe that He is using circumstances, both the good and the not-so-good, to make us more like Jesus. This is where we must trust the Lord in His perfect knowledge of us. He knows what ingredients need to be present in our lives to shape us into women or men after God's own heart. On the other hand, our worship and intimacy with the Lord are severely hindered when we allow pride, rebellion and unbelief to reign in our lives. The growth of our souls can seem imperceptible. I cannot tell you if I grew today or even yesterday. But when I look back over a period of time, I can see if I've gained or lost ground in my love relationship with Jesus.

Gordon MacDonald, in his book *The Life God Blesses*, states, "The life God blesses is marked by a tenacious desire to acquire an intimate knowledge of who He is." I see that so clearly in the life of Anna. We meet her when she is older but can catch meaningful glimpses of what her earlier years must have been like.

Here is Anna's story in Luke 2:36-38, an account of her meeting Simeon, Joseph, Mary, and the infant Jesus in the temple court:

> There was also a prophetess, Anna, the daughter of
> Phanuel, of the tribe of Asher. She was very old; she had
> lived with her husband seven years after her marriage,
> and then was a widow until she was eighty-four. She
> never left the temple but worshiped night and day,
> fasting and praying. Coming up to them at that very
> moment, she gave thanks to God and spoke about the
> child to all who were looking forward to the redemption
> of Jerusalem.

Luke uses six carefully chosen phrases to describe this godly older woman:

1. A PROPHETESS

She was one who foretold God's Word. Some have suggested that her husband was a prophet and when he died she took his place. It certainly speaks of her unusual closeness to God.

2. ANNA

Her name means favor or grace. And we shall discover that her name was lived out in her life.

3. THE DAUGHTER OF PHANUEL, OF THE TRIBE OF ASHER

Luke adds her heritage to his introduction to indicate her importance. Phanuel means the face, or appearance, of God. Asher means happiness. She would see the face of God in a little baby, and such a sight would bring great happiness to her and to all mankind.

4. VERY OLD

84, to be exact. Age in that culture was held in high regard.

5. MARRIED FOR SEVEN YEARS

She probably married when she was 12 to 14 years of age.

6. THEN BECAME A WIDOW

She had been alone since she was between 19 and 21 years of age.

I don't want to rush over these last three descriptions of Anna because they lend crucial insight into how God develops a life. It takes time and it involves trials. It has been said that salvation happens in an instant but the building of a saint takes a lifetime. I could not agree more. Most of us want to be godly . . . instantly.

Godliness is a life-long pursuit. At the moment Anna approached Simeon she did not know that the Savior had been born or that God was going to use her in such a significant way. She was just an old woman devoting herself to God the way she had for years. When you survey the Bible you'll see that God's work in a life is not hindered by age. Some of God's best servants were well advanced in years. Abraham was 75 years old when God originally

called him to go to the Promised Land and 100 years old before
the long-awaited Isaac was born. Moses was 80 years old when
God told him to go back and free His people from slavery. Caleb
was 85 when he asked Joshua for the hardest part of the Promised
Land for his own. And the apostle John was 90 when he received
the revelation of the end times in the last book of the Bible. Age
does not limit your journey down the Avenue to Worship.

But sadly, the Scripture is replete with examples of people who
began well and faded. Jonah never really got over his anger
with God's compassion that He showed to a sinful people.
Solomon came from a godly heritage and had a great start; but
he disobeyed the Lord and married foreign women and ended up
following their gods and not the one true God. Judas, a disciple,
turned Jesus over to His murderers for the price of a slave, 30
pieces of silver. Tragic endings to promising starts. Many of us
know people in our own corner of life who have made the same
horrid choices. Maybe you're one of them. It's never too late to
turn toward God and humbly ask for a fresh start.

- *Think about people you know who started strong
  and have since faded. Pray for them.*

- *Determine, with God's help, to remain strong
  until the end.*

- *Read what the apostle Paul said at the end of his
  life in 2 Timothy 4:6-8.*

I'm so glad we have the example of Anna who finished well.
She was an 84-year-old lover of God. When God was ready to
use her in a new way, she was ready to respond. What kind of
an older person do you want to be? What character qualities
do you want to have in your life? We must choose to submit
and embrace the development process *now*. We must be careful

not to be envious of others who are growing in their faith walk differently than we are. Our marching orders are to look to Jesus as the One who takes us down the Avenue to Worship. We may not reach our destination in an instant, but we will arrive in His perfect time.

- *Muse over Jude 24: "To him who is able to keep you from falling and to present you before his glorious presence without fault and with great joy—to the only God our Savior be glory, majesty, power and authority, through Jesus Christ our Lord, before all ages, now and forevermore! Amen.*

- *Thank God for such a great truth.*

Secondly, Anna's life was developed through *trials*. "She had lived with her husband seven years after her marriage, and then was a widow . . ." Sixteen little words to describe a world of pain, heartache and loss. Just hearing the word "widow" conjures up such sad feelings. To be a widow, a childless widow, in the Jewish culture was a place of loneliness and abandonment. Anna was just a young woman when she found herself without a husband, left with happy memories of what once was and a bleak prospect of what lay ahead—plans that were never fulfilled, dreams that were never realized and children that were never born. It was a life truncated before it even had time to begin.

- *Reflect on places of pain in your life.*

The trials you face may be vastly different from the one Anna faced. But you know what loss feels like, tastes like. The betrayal of a loved one, the rebellion of a teen, the waywardness of a spouse, or the loss of a job unfairly rocks our world and leaves us forever changed.

Why would God allow such times? The Bible does give us a few reasons. Trials in all their severity and dimensions are instruments God uses to make us like Jesus. When I am in the throes of a hard time, I try to remember three biblical promises that help me keep my perspective. First, there is a *purpose in trials*. Romans 5:2-4 tells us, "And we rejoice in the hope of the glory of God. Not only so, but we also rejoice in our sufferings, because we know that suffering produces perseverance; perseverance, character; and character, hope." Our challenge? To wait on God to do in us what can only be accomplished through this trial. Secondly, there are *perimeters around our trials*. 1 Peter 5:10-11 stresses this point well: "And the God of all grace, who called you to his eternal glory in Christ, after you have suffered a little while, will himself restore you and make you strong, firm and steadfast. To him be the power forever and ever. Amen." I am so thankful for this assurance. The challenge? Not to give up hope when the trials last longer than we think they should. Lastly, *praise eventually flows from our trials*. Listen to how 1 Peter 1:6-7 states it: "In this you greatly rejoice, though now for a little while you may have had to suffer grief in all kinds of trials. These have come so that your faith—of greater worth than gold, which perishes even though refined by fire—may be proved genuine and may result in praise, glory and honor when Jesus Christ is revealed." I have seen this truth played out in my life. My challenge is in continuing to give God permission to use the "fiery" times to purify my faith.

- *Choose one of the three verses listed above that brings you the most comfort and one that brings you the most challenge.*

- *Think about someone you need to share them with.*

I am impressed that early tragedy did not define the rest of Anna's life. She trusted God through the sleepless nights, the unanswered "why" questions, and the bottles and bottles of tears *He* promised to hold in His care (Psalm 56:8 NASB).

- *Have trials and troubles defined or derailed your life?*

Anna's life was developed over *time* and through *trials*. And our lives will be as well. So don't give up, give out or give in as you proceed down the Avenue to Worship. God wants to teach us about Himself when we trust Him in the difficult times. We learn how to go to His Word for comfort and strength, we learn to go deeper in prayer, and we experience more of His presence. In a word, we learn to *worship*. The sweet treasure of knowing Him better awaits those who persevere. Hudson Taylor's famous quote from *Spiritual Secrets* sums it up beautifully:

> It doesn't matter, really, how great the pressure is; it only matters where the pressure lies. See that it never comes between you and the Lord—then, the greater the pressure, the more it presses you to His breast.

- *Reflect on the pressures in your life.*

- *Consider if they are drawing you closer or pushing you away from the Lord.*

- *Analyze if your trials and troubles have taught you more about worshiping God.*

HER LIFE DEVOTED

Webster's Dictionary defines devote as "to set apart for a special purpose; to give up wholly; ardent love, affection and dedication." What a perfect description of Anna's life. Years of walking with God and the honing that happened through her widowhood produced an intimacy I want to emulate.

A.W. Tozer gives us needed insight into how we can follow in her footsteps:

> Pick at random a score of great saints whose lives and testimonies are widely known. Let them be Bible characters or well-known Christians of post-biblical times. You will be struck instantly with the fact that the saints were not alike . . . I venture to suggest that the one vital quality which they had in common was spiritual receptivity. Something in them was open to heaven, something which urged them Godward . . . They had spiritual awareness and they went on to cultivate it until it became the biggest thing in their lives. They differed from the average person in that when they felt the inward longing they *did something about it.* They acquired the lifelong habit of spiritual response. (*Pursuit of God*)

Anna's life was characterized by spiritual receptivity. Instead of getting angry with God, bitter toward life and others who did not have her same set of circumstances, she devoted herself to the *presence of God.* We learn from the text that Anna never left the temple. It was her literal home and her spiritual home. She probably had a room in the women's section of the temple. I am not aware of another woman in the Bible who had such an honored residence. It seems she wanted to be close to the Lord because He had been so close to her when the bottom fell out of her life.

She also devoted herself to the *praise of God*. Luke tells us that she "worshiped day and night, fasting and praying." Each one of these practices was a Spirit-inspired action that flowed from her love. Where love is meager worship will wane. So it's no surprise that Anna had a life of worship. For Luke to describe this practice as continual speaks volumes of her devotion and godly reputation. I think Richard Foster has it right: "To be effective pray-ers, we need to be effective lovers . . . Real prayer comes not from gritting our teeth but from falling in love" *(Prayer: Finding the Heart's True Home)*. Fasting is about seeking the Lord. The Old and New Testaments record this well-worn habit, practiced by men and women who abstained from food for up to 40 days. The goal? Increased intimacy with God.

There is much about Anna's life that is vastly different from mine: her age, widowhood, childlessness and cloistered life. But her humility, surrender and devotion are qualities still needed in our day. How do we make fresh strides in these godly qualities? Let me suggest a method that has been most helpful to me. I call it the "ABC's of Devotion:"

Abide—In John 15 (NASB) we are commanded seven times by Jesus to abide in Him. This means we are to make our home in Him. How do we do that? We must be mindful of Him at all times. We must talk to Him about everything that is important to us. We must enjoy His presence. What does this look like in our daily lives? Well, for me it means that I am talking to God throughout my day. I talk with Him about the people I am with and the places I go. I tell Him my worries and fears and about the things that put a smile on my face. I try to memorize Bible verses so I can have an attitude of praise in my inner world.

Bottom line, when we abide in Christ He is a part of all we do. This will take practice, to be sure, but the rewards will include a significant increase in our devotion to the Lord.

- **Read John 15.**

- **Evaluate how you will keep the Lord more a part of your daily life.**

Behold—Isaiah 40:10 (NASB) tells us to "Behold, the Lord God . . . " Beholding the Lord involves spending time in His Word and prayer. It is the habit of seeing the Lord in the issues we wrestle with. For example, if I am finding it hard to believe God loves me, I turn to 1 John 3:1-3 and pray the truth of those verses into my life. I also like finding biblical characters who experienced difficulties similar to my own. If I am struggling to believe God's forgiveness after I sin, I am encouraged when I see how Jesus dealt with Peter's denial in John 21.

- **Think about the issues you've been chewing on lately.**

- **Consider verses or biblical characters that could help you bring God into the concerns.**

Celebrate—Abiding and beholding the LORD are quiet, internal practices that lead to the need to celebrate. Psalm 95:1 tells us, "Come, let us sing for joy to the Lord; let us shout aloud to the Rock of our salvation." I spend a great deal of time in the Psalms learning the language of praise. Our walk with the Lord should be punctuated with a real spirit of celebration for all the Lord has done for us. We praise the Lord not because He needs it, but because we do. We become like the One we praise. Celebrate well and celebrate often!

Avenue to
Worship

Following Him

When I Can't See
the End of the Road

102

• *Open to Psalm 98. Read one verse at a time and then pray the contents of the verse back to the Lord.*

HIS LIFE DECLARED

Anna's life was well-pleasing to the Lord. She submitted to the developmental process that He chose for her, she devoted her life to Him, and now she was ready to be used by Him in a most significant way. The last time she is mentioned in the Bible is in Luke 2:38: "Coming up to them at that very moment, she gave thanks to God and spoke about the child to all who were looking forward to the redemption of Jerusalem." The Spirit of God brought Anna out to the temple courts at the moment when Simeon, Joseph and Mary were dedicating baby Jesus. Her first response was one of thanksgiving. I would love to have heard that prayer. It seems that she knew what was going on. The Savior had come and was in her presence! She'd spent her life worshiping the invisible God and now He had come in the flesh and was right there with her. What a thrilling moment it must have been for her.

Her second response was to tell the other people in Jerusalem that Messiah had come. She was the first female missionary in the New Testament. This godly, older woman was ready to be used by God to bring the Good News to others waiting to hear. What an honor!

It is the same for us today. The more we know and love the Lord, the more inclined we will be to tell others about Him. Mike Barton says it well: "Our responsibility is to take a good look at Jesus and tell others what we see."

- *Make a list of people you know who need to come to know Jesus as their Savior.*

- *Begin to pray daily for them.*

Progressing down the Avenue to Worship means we need to *stay submitted* to Him. When God convicts, respond. When He calls, act. And when He speaks, listen. Ruth Harms Calkin expresses this well:

Lord, I thought I had
Given myself to You irrevocably.
I mean it, Lord.
I honestly thought
There would be no turning back
No secret side glances.
But now I shamefully hang my head:
I'm bewildered
I'm chagrined
By the frightening discovery
Of my unlimited capacity
For self-indulgence.
I'm beginning to understand
That my surrender must be
Moment-by-moment
As well as once-for-all.
(Lord, You Love to Say Yes)

- *Pause to pray about your submission.*

*Avenue to
Worship*

Following Him

*When I Can't See
the End of the Road*

104

We also need to *stay supple*. Ask God to protect you from the hard heart, the stiff neck and a brazen will. God wants us to be soft and pliable in His hands so He can mold us and shape us into the man or woman most pleasing in His sight.

- ***Pause to pray about your softness toward the Lord.***

Finally, make it your aim to *stay strong* all the way to the end. We all will fall down and skin our spiritual knees but, by God's grace and help, we'll get up and keep going. Just think if Anna had allowed the death of her husband to take her out of the race. She would have missed out on all that God had in store for her in her elderly years.

- ***Pause and pray about walking with the Lord for your whole life.***

Anna left her footsteps for us to follow along the Avenue to Worship.

Meditations for the Journey
WORSHIP

Consider . . .

God's Word

> "Holy, holy, holy is the LORD Almighty; the whole earth
> is full of his glory."
>
> **Isaiah 6:3**

> They fell down on their faces before the throne and
> worshiped God, saying,
> > "Amen!
> > Praise and glory
> > and wisdom and thanks and honor
> > and power and strength
> > be to our God for ever and ever.
> > Amen!"
>
> **Revelation 7:11-12**

God's Heart

> O My child, I need thee for Myself. Yea, I have purposes
> for thy life beyond thy present comprehension. Yea, I have
> truth concerning Myself to give to thee, deeper and richer
> and more wonderful than thine understanding has thus
> far taken in.

*Meditations
for the Journey*
Worship

Following Him

*When I Can't See
the End of the Road*

106

Open thine heart wide to Me. I will fill thee with My Holy
Spirit, and in doing so will satisfy the deepest longings of
thy soul.

Frances J. Roberts, *Come Away, My Beloved*

Singing . . .

O Worship the King

*O worship the King, all glorious above, and gratefully sing
His pow'r and His love; our Shield and Defender, the Ancient
of Days, pavilioned in splendor and girded with praise.*

*O tell of His might, O sing of His grace, whose robe is the light,
whose canopy space; His chariots of wrath the deep thunderclouds
form, and dark is His path on the wings of the storm.*

*Frail children of dust, and feeble as frail, in thee do we trust,
nor find thee to fail; Thy mercies how tender, how firm to
the end! Our Maker, Defender, Redeemer and Friend.*

Robert Grant, 1779-1838

Praying . . .

*What an awesome God You are, Precious Lord and King!
The question posed by the psalmist comes to my mind,
"Who can proclaim the mighty acts of the* LORD *or fully
declare his praise?" (Psalm 106:2) No one! My words
fall short and my vocabulary is so limited when it comes to
praising You. Please, teach me the language of praise and
enable me to worship You in spirit and truth.* **Amen.**

> *"In forgiveness . . . we are inviting our offenders*
> *back into the circle of fellowship."*
>
> **Richard Foster,**
> *Prayer: Finding the Heart's True Home*

Avenue to FORGIVENESS

The sadness in Connie's face signaled urgency, and the pitiful tone in her voice pierced my heart when she asked if I had time to talk with her. We made our way to a private spot and she proceeded to tell me her sad story. The previous week, amidst the joy and excitement of preparing to come to the women's retreat, Connie had discovered that her husband was hopelessly addicted to pornography, and as a result had met a woman in an Internet chat room. One tragic mistake led to another, and they eventually met and slept together.

Connie's husband, a Christian, filled with guilt and remorse, had confessed the whole sordid affair to her and begged her not to leave him. She was unable to sleep, unable to eat, but mostly unable to forgive. She was hurt and wanted to hurt him back. God used my words to flood her heart and mind with the need to forgive her husband. Sobbing, she asked what she should do next. I asked her if we could pray for God's wisdom. Questions such as Connie's are far outside my ability to answer. As soon as I said "Amen," the Lord brought a few biblical principles to mind. First was the example of Jesus our Savior. While hanging on

Avenue to
Forgiveness

Following Him

*When I Can't See
the End of the Road*

108

the cross, covered with the spit of His accusers, He said,
"Father, forgive them, for they do not know what they are doing"
(Luke 23:34). The apostle Peter, in his first epistle, tells us what
was going on in Jesus' heart while He was saying these words:
"When they hurled their insults at him, he did not retaliate;
when he suffered, he made no threats. Instead, he entrusted
himself to him who judges justly" (I Peter 2:23). I told Connie
that she must lean deeply into the heart and words of Jesus to
forgive her husband. Jesus did not fight back, He did not look
for a way to get even . . . He forgave and trusted God to do the
judging. The same Lord of forgiveness lives within her and He'd
help her to perform the same supernatural act of forgiveness.

The second principle that popped into my mind came from
Ephesians 4:32, "Be kind and compassionate to one another,
forgiving each other, just as in Christ God forgave you." We
forgive because we have been forgiven. We will always live with
the consequences of another's sin whether we want to or not. The
question is will we live in the freedom of forgiveness or in the
bondage of unforgiveness? It is impossible, Connie and I agreed,
to do this on our own. Only as God gives us grace and strength
can we extend forgiveness to one who has broken our heart and
damaged our trust.

We prayed together again and through her tears, she chose to
forgive her husband. She told me she would write me when
she returned home, so you can imagine my joy when I actually
received her letter. She recounted the initial conversation with her
husband, how they had cried, and the marriage counsel they had
eventually received. It had not been easy or quick, but she could
honestly say that their marriage was better than ever. She was
amazed at God's great love and grace. Connie was well on her
way down the Avenue to Forgiveness.

Connie's story is not unique. Sadly, I hear many variations of this same scenario as I teach around the country. You too may have a situation in your life when it's been hard, even impossible, to forgive. The list could go on and on, couldn't it? Parents who rejected you, a child who has run away, a violent crime against yourself or a loved one, your own personal failures that haunt you constantly?

- *Consider whether you have forgiven the offense.*

- *Choose to ask God to help you forgive based on the Scriptures I used in counseling the woman at the retreat.*

- *Seek help from a pastor, friend or professional counselor if you are struggling with unforgiveness. God wants you to be free from the pain of past offenses.*

I am forever grateful for a God who forgives and forgives. He graciously invites us to come to Him in whatever condition we may be. Ruth Senter penned a delightful prayer that expresses this truth so well:

I came to You sad.

You did not say, "Be happy."

Instead,

You cried with me;

My tears rolled down Your cheeks

So great was Your love/pain for me.

I did not have to be anything when I came to You

But me.

I came to You frazzled.

Avenue to
Forgiveness

Following Him

When I Can't See
the End of the Road

110

You did not say, "Be calm."

Instead,

You took my hand and said,

"Tell me about it . . . "

I told You

And in the telling I was calmed.

I did not have to be anything when I came to You

But me.

I came to You absorbed in myself.

You did not say, "You're too introspective."

Instead,

You waited around

Until I could reach beyond myself,

Until I was released from myself.

I did not have to be anything when I came to You

But me.

I came to You just as I was.

You welcomed me into Your arms.

You gave me myself,

And the gift was priceless.

(*Longing for Love*)

- *Pause and pray.*

- *Remember a time when you came to God with a big need.*

- *Thank Him for being there for you.*

There is a quiet woman in Luke's gospel who came to the Savior just as she was. No small matter for a prostitute! She had more reasons to stay away from Him than to go find Him dining at a local Pharisee's home. The religious people had always treated her with such disgust and disdain. She was sure God felt that way about her, too. But word had reached her that this Jesus was different from other rabbis. He was willing to touch the unclean, forgive the blatant sinner and eat with tax collectors. Perhaps she'd heard Him teach; maybe she'd talked to a healed leper or witnessed the blind receiving sight. We don't know the details. We can conclude that she had heard or seen enough to really believe it would be safe to come into His presence uninvited to express her love.

It is unclear from the story, found only in Luke 7:36-50, whether she came to faith prior to this meeting or during her encounter with Jesus. But she came with determination to express her gratitude and left esteemed by God Himself. She knew she was desperate to find the on-ramp to the Avenue to Forgiveness. Something in her told her she had to get to Jesus. He'd know the way.

Her loving humility is contrasted with the prideful Simon, the Pharisee, who had invited Jesus over for dinner and had concluded he had no need for such a Savior. Consequently, he never began his journey down the Avenue to Forgiveness. But more on that later. For now, let's take a closer look at our needy

Avenue to
Forgiveness

Following Him

When I Can't See
the End of the Road

112

woman.

HER PAINFUL PAST

Luke leaves little doubt about this woman's citywide
reputation. Four times in 14 verses we are told she was a sinner
(Luke 7:37, 39, 47, 48). Luke tells us in verse 37 she "lived a
sinful life." Simon recognizes the same fact in verse 39, that "she
is a sinner." And even Jesus in verse 47 tells the whole dinner
party, "Therefore, I tell you, her many sins have been forgiven."
Jesus expresses this sentiment again in verse 48, "Your sins are
forgiven." My friend, she was a sinner with a messy past!

Most scholars agree she was almost certainly a prostitute. It's clear
from the text that all in the dining room knew who she was and
what she did. Her presence in a Pharisee's home was shocking.
We must keep in mind the customary male prejudices against
women at this time. No man would have spoken in public to any
woman other than his own wife, certainly not a prostitute!

Not so with Jesus. Everyone found a place with Him. The culture
and the religion of this woman's day may have cast her aside, but
not the Lord. Only in the Bible would you find the prostitute
gaining audience with the pristine one. He never flinched when
she touched Him. He was not appalled by her but accepting of her
love. Jesus welcomed sinners and she was no exception. God gives
where He finds empty hands, and hers had been empty for so long.

Unless I miss my guess, each of us has painful pasts filled with
poor choices and even questionable reputations. Your past may
hold obvious mistakes that everyone can see or a whole slew of
missteps no one is privy to. Makes no difference. God sees it all
and wants to forgive it all. If we desire to make progress down
the Avenue to Forgiveness we must begin by being honest with
God about our sins . . . past or present. A practice I employ when
it's been a while since I've been straight with God is to make a sin

list. This is how it works. I start with prayer: "Lord, it's been a while since I've come into Your presence, and I am hurting. I have said or done some things that are not right. Your Word says if I confess my sins, You are faithful and just and will forgive me my sins and purify me from all unrighteousness (1 John 1:9). Help me to be honest with You so I can experience Your forgiveness." Then I take a sheet of paper and write down anything and everything that comes to mind. One of the ministries of the Holy Spirit is to convict us of our sin, so you can be sure that if there are things clogging up your relationship with God, He will bring them to mind (John 16:8). When I am done, I literally write out 1 John 1:9 over the top of the list. I then thank God I am forgiven, not because I *feel* forgiven but because His Word says that I am.

*Avenue to
Forgiveness*

Following Him

*When I Can't See
the End of the Road*

113

- *Determine if you need to make a sin list.*

- *End your time with God by reading Psalm 19:12-13. "Who can discern his errors? Forgive my hidden faults. Keep your servant also from willful sins; may they not rule over me. Then will I be blameless, innocent of great transgression."*

HER PASSIONATE PURSUIT

As we look again at the woman in Luke 7, we see that her keen awareness of her past only enhanced the passion with which she pursued her Savior. He offered all she needed most . . . love, acceptance, forgiveness and a new start in life. Verses 37-38 set the stage.

> When a woman who had lived a sinful life in that town learned that Jesus was eating at the Pharisee's house, she brought an alabaster jar of perfume, and as she stood

Avenue to
Forgiveness

Following Him

When I Can't See
the End of the Road

114

behind him at his feet weeping, she began to wet his feet with her tears. Then she wiped them with her hair, kissed them and poured perfume on them.

When this sinful woman heard where Jesus was located, she had to go be with Him. But she did much more than simply enjoy His presence. I counted six ways in which she reached out in love to Him.

1. She stood behind Him by his feet. It is important to note that the customary position for dinner guests would be to lie on couches with their heads near the table, propping themselves up on one elbow and stretching their legs out behind them. The table itself was only about two feet off the ground. It seems that she entered the room right behind Jesus. I picture her tentative at first, very much aware of all the disapproving eyes on her.

2. She was weeping. I wonder if she expected to cry so hard? I think the mere sight of her Savior caused the recesses of her soul to open with great sobs of repentance and sorrow over her sin.

3. She began to wet His feet with her tears. By now she must have been on her knees so that the abundance of her tears could fall on Jesus' feet. She was actually washing the Lord's feet with her own tears! What a magnificent scene of humility and love. For many years I never quite understood how enough tears could be produced to wet feet. Then a few years ago I was involved in a church conference where women were moved to confess their sins to one another. It was a very precious time. As I stood in a circle praying for these dear ones who were finally finding release from hidden sins, my shoes filled up with their tears. It made this section of Scripture come alive for me.

4. She wiped His feet with her hair. Another sign of grateful affection. A woman of that culture normally would not have unbound her hair in public.

5. She kissed His feet. Now fully bowed down in His presence so her lips could reach His feet, she showed a love beyond description.

6. She poured perfume on His feet. It came from an alabaster jar. Many Jewish women wore a small container of perfume around their necks. These jars were beautiful and the perfume expensive. Caring for the feet of a guest was the job of a slave. Again, she was showing profound humility and thankfulness to Jesus.

Each of these six actions speaks loudly of this woman's passion for God. Her pursuit is filled with tenderness, brokenness over sin and sacrificial service to her God. He was Messiah, Emmanuel, God With Us. Would any other response do? Through her we witness a holy moment of uninhibited love.

May I ask a few probing questions? How passionate is your pursuit of God? Are you more in love with Him today than you were six months ago, a year ago, five years ago? Is His Word food for your soul? Do you spend time just telling Him about what's on your heart? Has there ever been a time when you were overcome with gratitude for all the ways God has forgiven you? What can you do differently to ensure continued growth? Making progress on the Avenue to Forgiveness necessitates that we be diligent in our pursuit of God. Why? Because the more we love Him, the more sensitive we will be to stay away from *anything* that would hinder our fellowship with Him.

- *Endeavor to rate your "diligence factor."*
- *Determine if change needs to occur.*
- *Consider the attitudes or actions that seem to consistently trip you up.*

*Avenue to
Forgiveness*

Following Him

*When I Can't See
the End of the Road*

116

• *Pray that you'd stand strong in these areas with
  God's help.*

HER PESKY PERSECUTOR

Throughout Jesus' visit in Simon's home, the host remained
haughty and hardened toward Jesus and toward the woman. His
haughtiness is seen in a couple of ways. Our first introduction to
Simon is in Luke 7:36, when he invited Jesus to have dinner with
him. It was a traditional practice for a local Pharisee to invite a
traveling rabbi over for a meal. But what is not mentioned at the
top of the story is how Simon neglected to care for his guest in a
proper way. If your Bible is open, look at verses 44-46:

> Then he turned toward the woman and said to Simon,
> "Do you see this woman? I came into your house. You
> did not give me any water for my feet, but she wet my
> feet with her tears and wiped them with her hair. You
> did not give me a kiss, but this woman, from the time I
> entered, has not stopped kissing my feet. You did not put
> oil on my head, but she has poured perfume on my feet."

Quite a scathing rebuke! Why would Simon have a guest
for dinner and omit the common courtesies? My guess? His
pompous pride prevented him from extending any kindness. I
think he saw himself as morally superior and even a cut above
Jesus. Perhaps that's why he treated Him with disrespect right
from the start. The unnamed woman loved and dearly treasured
the Lord, and her acts showed the true condition of her heart . . .
and so did Simon's.

The second indication of haughtiness is found in verse 39,
"When the Pharisee who had invited him saw this, [that Jesus
allowed himself to be touched by the sinner woman] he said

to himself, 'If this man were a prophet, he would know who is touching him and what kind of woman she is—that she is a sinner.' " What a contrast in response! Jesus was welcoming and accepting of the woman's love as evidence of a changed life. You'd think the town Pharisee would be delighted that a "woman of the street" had changed her ways. Not so with Simon. He greeted her with sarcasm and contempt.

Yes, God gives where He finds empty hands, but Simon's were too full of self-righteousness to receive anything. It takes a contrite heart to receive forgiveness and admit the need for a Savior. Simon had no time for either. The Avenue to Forgiveness was fine for others, but he was sure he didn't need to take such a journey. A few chapters later, in Luke 18:9-14, the contrast between a prideful heart and a humble one is vividly portrayed:

117

> To some who were confident of their own righteousness and looked down on everybody else, Jesus told this parable: "Two men went up to the temple to pray, one a Pharisee and the other a tax collector. The Pharisee stood up and prayed about himself: 'God, I thank you that I am not like other men—robbers, evildoers, adulterers—or even like this tax collector. I fast twice a week and give a tenth of all I get.' But the tax collector stood at a distance. He would not even look up to heaven, but beat his breast and said, 'God have mercy on me, a sinner.' I tell you that this man, rather than the other, went home justified before God. For everyone who exalts himself will be humbled, and he who humbles himself will be exalted."

- ***Select one of the characters in the parable with whom you identify more.***

Here we have the prideful heart exposed by Jesus . . . haughty, self-righteous, puffed up with its own good deeds and quick to look down on others. It stands in stark contrast to the humility and brokenness of the tax collector in this parable and the woman in the Luke 7 story we have been exploring.

Not only was Simon haughty but he also had a hard, unteachable heart. In Luke 7:40-43, Jesus told him a story about two men in debt to a moneylender. One owed the lender 500 denarii, and the other 50. These were both very large debts, because one denarius coin was worth a day's wages. The moneylender chose to forgive both the debts. Jesus then posed a question to Simon: "Now, which of them will love him [the lender] more?" Simon replied, "I suppose the one who had the bigger debt canceled." Jesus told him that he had answered correctly.

I am amazed by the grace of Jesus. With love and a longing for Simon to come to the end of himself, He told a story, hoping it would crack Simon's hardened heart. But pride prevented Simon from making the personal application that the woman had already made. He simply saw no need for Jesus. The woman knew she was the sinner forgiven much; therefore she could love in unrestricted ways. Simon's haughty and hardened heart could only scorn and look away. Prideful people always minimize their own sin and maximize others'. Simon had the Messiah at his dinner table and did not recognize Him. He didn't see his own huge spiritual need, and he turned away in smug self-righteousness, never receiving what Jesus longed to give—the forgiveness of sin.

God is intolerant of the calloused heart. He is patient with our mistakes. He is longsuffering with our stumbles. He doesn't get angry at our questions. He doesn't turn away when we struggle. But when we repeatedly reject His message, when we are insensitive to His pleadings, when He changes history itself to get our attention and we still don't listen, He honors our request. (Max Lucado, *And the Angels were Silent*)

- *Acknowledge any place where you have not listened to God.*

- *Ask Him to soften your heart and protect you from smug self-righteousness.*

Simon may have been belittling our female friend, but Jesus was not. Four times during His interchange with the Pharisee He esteemed her. In verse 44 Jesus' words are profound, "Then he *turned toward the woman* and said to Simon . . . " (italics added). The Lord used this woman's actions as a perfect example of how He should have been treated in Simon's home. Again, in verses 47 and 48, in front of all the guests, Jesus announced that her sins were forgiven and then gave the reason for her loving outpour to Him: "Her many sins have been forgiven—for she loved much." Her love did not earn her forgiveness; rather, she loved because she was forgiven. And lastly, in verse 50, He gently dismissed this dear one, saying, "Your faith has saved you; go in peace." He became her defender, her forgiver and her peace.

There are more than a few lessons to be learned from this biblical story. Do we overestimate our own righteousness? Are we guilty of seeing ourselves as a cut above people of other cultures or skin color? Are we prideful? These may not be easy questions

Avenue to
Forgiveness

Following Him

*When I Can't See
the End of the Road*

120

to answer, but they must be looked at if we hope to stay on the Avenue to Forgiveness. Sin is subtle and can find many places in our heart to hide. Pride is a sin that can go undetected. Be willing to take a long, hard look at yourself.

James, the Lord's half brother, tells us, "God opposes the proud but gives grace to the humble. Submit yourselves, then, to God. Resist the devil, and he will flee from you. Come near to God and he will come near to you" (James 4:6-8). James pinpoints a few steps we can take to ensure that we keep a humble heart. First, realize how God feels about pride and humility. Secondly, submit to God. That is, do what He requires regardless of how you may feel. If it's God's will it is always the best choice. Next, stand against the devil's ways and he will hightail it out of your life. Lastly, run into God's extended arms of love for you. Humility is another key aspect to our trek down the Avenue to Forgiveness.

The woman of Luke 7 had quite an evening, didn't she? We can only speculate as to how she must have felt. Her life would never be the same. She'd been forgiven, loved, and esteemed by God in the flesh. God gives where He finds empty hands, and she left full—full of peace, God's peace. I love how Philippians 4:7 describes this peace (Amplified Bible):

> And God's peace [shall be yours, that tranquil state of a soul assured of its salvation through Christ, and so fearing nothing from God and being content with its earthly lot of whatever sort that is, that peace] which transcends all understanding shall garrison and mount guard over your hearts and minds in Christ Jesus.

She came to see Jesus. *That's where it all began.* She beheld His
beauty and perfection and came away with a whole new life.
No longer a woman of the streets but now a daughter of the
King and a child of God. Has He done any less for you and me?
Perhaps the woman remains unnamed because we are to put
our name in her place. We come from a life of rebellion, ruin
and ruckus. We've been cleansed deeper than we ever thought
possible so that we, too, may experience a similar passion,
intimacy and devotion to the Lord. The Avenue to Forgiveness
is wide enough to accommodate every traveler who wants a fresh
touch from Jesus.

Richard Foster's book *Prayers from the Heart* contains a passage
I'd like you to personalize.

> Clean out, O God, the inner steam of my life:
>> All the duplicity,
>>
>> All the avarice,
>>
>> All the falsity.

> Search out, O Lord, the hidden motives of my life:
>> All the conceit,
>>
>> All the anger,
>>
>> All the fear.

Root out, divine Master, the destructive actions of my life:

All manipulations,

All the scheming,

All the guile.

May the operations of faith, hope, and love increase in Everything I am and in everything I do.

Amen.

FORGIVENESS

Consider . . .

God's Word

> *Who is a God like you, who pardons sin and forgives the*
> *transgression of the remnant of his inheritance?*
> *You do not stay angry forever but delight to show mercy.*
>
> **Micah 7:18**

> *Then the Lord came down in the cloud and . . . he passed*
> *in front of Moses, proclaiming, "The LORD, the LORD, the*
> *compassionate and gracious God, slow to anger, abounding*
> *in love and faithfulness, maintaining love to thousands,*
> *and forgiving wickedness, rebellion and sin."*
>
> **Exodus 34:5-7**

God's Heart

> *Thank You, LORD, for cleansing my heart's wound with Living*
> *Water. Thank You for Your bandage of pure, gentle love.*
> *Thank You for the kiss of comfort. At last the hurt is gone.*

Ruth Harms Calkin, *Tell Me Again, Lord, I Forget*

*Meditations
for the Journey
Forgiveness*

Following Him

*When I Can't See
the End of the Road*

Singing . . .

Nothing But the Blood

*What can wash away my sin? Nothing but the blood of Jesus.
What can make me whole again? Nothing but the
blood of Jesus.*

*For my pardon this I see—nothing but the blood of Jesus. For
my cleansing, this my plea—nothing but the blood of Jesus.*

*This is all my hope and peace—nothing but the blood of Jesus.
This is all my righteousness—nothing but the blood of Jesus.*

*Refrain: Oh! Precious is the flow that makes me white as
snow. No other fount I know—nothing but the blood of Jesus.*

Robert Lowry, 1826-1899

Praying . . .

*You found me at my worst and gave me Your best. You
have freed me from my guilt and shame . . . all those things
that even now, when I think about them, make me blush.
You did not turn away from me but came toward me,
offering me pardon, cleansing through the blood of Jesus,
and a whole new life. I took Your gift and have never been
the same. Thank You, dearest Friend.*

"Wisdom is the acquired ability to live life well. It's living life against the grindstone and coming away polished instead of being chewed up. It is when our mistakes and failures become our teachers."

David Swartz,
Dancing with Broken Bones

Avenue to WISDOM

At the turn of the 20th century there was an asylum in the suburbs of Boston which housed severely challenged individuals. One of the patients was a girl who was simply called Little Annie. She was totally unresponsive to others in the asylum. The staff tried everything they could to help her, yet without success. Finally she was confined to a cell in the basement of the asylum and given up as hopeless.

But a beautiful Christian woman worked at the asylum, and she believed that every one of God's creatures needed love, concern and care. So she decided to spend her lunch hours in front of Little Annie's cell, reading to her and praying that God would free her from the prison of silence. Day after day the Christian woman came to Little Annie's door and read, but the girl made no response. Months went by. The woman tried to talk with Little Annie, but it was like talking to an empty cell. She brought little tokens of food for the girl, but they were never received. Then one day a brownie was missing from the plate which the caring woman retrieved from Little Annie's cell. Encouraged, she continued to read to her and pray for her. Eventually the little girl began to answer the woman through the bars of her cell. Soon the woman convinced the doctors that Little Annie needed a second chance at treatment. They brought her up from the basement and continued to work with her. Within two years Little Annie was told that she could leave the asylum and enjoy a normal life.

But she chose not to leave. She was so grateful for the love and attention she was given by the dedicated Christian woman that she decided to stay and love others, as she had been loved. So Annie stayed on at the institution to work with other patients who were suffering as she had suffered.

Nearly half a century later, the Queen of England held a special ceremony to honor one of America's most inspiring women, Helen Keller. When asked to what she would attribute her success at overcoming the dual handicap of blindness and deafness, Helen Keller replied, "If it hadn't been for Ann Sullivan, I wouldn't be here today."

Ann Sullivan, who tenaciously loved and believed in an incorrigible blind and deaf girl named Helen Keller, was Little Annie. Because one selfless Christian woman in the dungeon of an insane asylum believed that a hopeless little girl needed God's love, the world received the marvelous gift of Helen Keller. (source and author unknown)

What an incredible picture of wisdom in action! The Christian woman who had such an impact on Annie's life as a child saw beyond the silent girl hiding in a dark cell. She was determined to act out God's love in a situation that seemed hopeless. Her choice made a huge impact on Annie's life and on the life of a woman

Avenue to
Wisdom

Following Him

When I Can't See
the End of the Road

127

yet to be born, Helen Keller. That's what wisdom is all about. It is knowledge lived out in our everyday world. It is putting into practice what the Lord says is true. The book of Proverbs tells us that real wisdom doesn't come from us but from God. "For the LORD gives wisdom, and from his mouth come knowledge and understanding" (Proverbs 2:6).

How can we be wise people? What is needed for us to make real progress down the Avenue to Wisdom? A few things come to mind that are crucial underpinnings to becoming people of wisdom. First, we need to know God personally, not just be a church attender or moral citizen. We must be intimately connected to God through a personal relationship with Jesus Christ. And this relationship must be cultivated so it can grow into the most important aspect of our lives. We need a dovetail relationship with God. What do I mean by that? Well, you are probably familiar with the way furniture manufacturers cut the wood for drawers or cabinets in such a way that the pieces fit together tightly without need of nails, glue or staples. That's how I picture my relationship with Jesus. All the various aspects of my life . . . career, family, friends, vacations, hidden hurts, secret dreams . . . need to be deeply and tightly connected with who God is. When this is happening, I am growing as a Christian because He is a part of all I do. But there have been times when I have not been well connected with Him. I've forgotten Him and His promises and gone my own way. The result? A distance and a separation that are only corrected when I determine to turn around and go His way.

- *Decide if you have a dovetail relationship with Him.*

- *Determine if you need a course correction.*

Secondly, if we want to be persons of wisdom, we need to be falling more and more in love with God. The quality of our love is seen in the way we act. Jesus consistently links obedience and love together in rather remarkable ways. Read one of the Gospels this week and notice how uncompromisingly Jesus obeyed His Father as an expression of His love. Never forget that we have a Father in heaven who is crazy about us (1 John 4:7-18) and wants nothing more than to see us live a full and abundant life (John 10:10), a life free of all the habits and addictions that ruin and destroy (Galatians 5:19-21). Who wouldn't want to obey a God like that?

- *Read the verses listed above.*

- *Thank the Lord for such a love.*

- *Ask Him to help you love Him better.*

Lastly, to be a person of wisdom we must live our lives as Jesus did . . . submissively, humbly, wisely and as a servant. I agree with what Wesley Duewel once said, "To become a person of God we must spend much time with Jesus. The more you love Him, the more you will want to spend time with Him. A weak prayer life always testifies to a weak love for Jesus. You cannot have a merely nominal or casual prayer life when you are passionately devoted to the Lord. The more you are with Him, the more you will think and speak like Him, respond and resemble Him. You will be a person of God." *(Ablaze for God)*

- *Recommit to being a person of God.*

The biblical woman who will lead us down the Avenue to Wisdom knew God intimately, loved Him passionately and followed Him wholeheartedly in what you will see was a very difficult situation. Abigail truly lived life against a grindstone and came away polished instead of being chewed up. The Bible text we will consider describes her as "an intelligent and beautiful woman." But all was not well in her world. She shared her home with a husband whose cruelty and foolishness were well-known throughout the region. Although neither her culture nor her husband held her in high regard, she consistently demonstrated tact, skill and wisdom. I like thinking of this story as the biblical version of Beauty and the Beast. Abigail is the beauty in both form and character from the beginning to the end, and her husband is the beast: mean, selfish and unkind.

She was born about 1,000 years before Christ and resided in the mountainous country of Judah in the town of Carmel. The longest account of her life is found in the Old Testament book of 1 Samuel 25. (Don't be too shy to look at the table of contents at the beginning of the Bible to help you find this or any other book in the Bible.) It is a long passage, so it would be best if you could grab a Bible and read it for yourself. We will take our time in this lush section of God's Word. Abigail's wisdom and godly character are not so much described as demonstrated in her dealings with two men headed for disaster.

HER PROBLEM

Problems are a part of every day and every generation. I keep waiting for a time when they are gone. And you know what? There will be such a time: HEAVEN! But until then, I best get a grip on how to handle difficulties God's way. That's why I like Abigail. She had not one major problem, but two. And as you shall see, they were huge, life-changing ones. Even so, she navigated through them with such grace and godliness.

- *Pinpoint a problem you are facing today.*

- *Note Abigail's methods and strategies.*

- *Consider if any are applicable to your situation.*

Abigail's first problem lived under her own roof: her husband Nabal. Each time he is described in this chapter, it is in rather unsavory terms:

Verse 3—"surly and mean in his dealings."

Verses 10-11—(Nabal speaking) "Who is this David? Who is this son of Jesse? Many servants are breaking away from their masters these days. Why should I take my bread and water, and the meat I have slaughtered for my shearers, and give it to men coming from who knows where?" Here we see the selfish, surly and mean side of Nabal coming out in full force. A little background is needed here. David had cared for these very shearers of Nabal's as they worked in the region where David and his 600 men lived. David had provided protection for them so, in a very real way, part of Nabal's prosperity was on account of David's kindness. Plus, to so rudely refuse weary travelers was unthinkable in that culture. Hospitality of the day demanded that food and water be given to any group, no matter the size. This conflict is at the heart of the problem Abigail had to negotiate on her husband's behalf, because when this common courtesy was denied, David and his men went ballistic! Nabal's rude reply caused David's blood to boil. His thinking probably went something like this, "How dare this man

Avenue to
Wisdom

Following Him

When I Can't See
the End of the Road

131

treat my men with such contempt! We shall see how he responds when I come to him uninvited and kill his whole household!" (See verse 17.) But more on that later.

Verse 14—"One of the servants told Nabal's wife Abigail: 'David sent messengers from the desert to give our master his greetings, but he hurled insults at them.'"

Verse 17— (servant speaking) "He is such a wicked man that no one can talk to him."

Verse 25— (Abigail speaking) "May my lord [David] pay no attention to that wicked man Nabal. He is just like his name—his name is Fool, and folly goes with him."

There is not a single nice thing said about this man in all forty-four verses of this chapter. David had extended a real act of kindness, and all of Nabal's servants recognized what David had done. One of these servants told Abigail about David's actions in verses 15-16. "These men were very good to us. They did not mistreat us, and the whole time we were out in the fields near them nothing was missing. Night and day they were a wall around us all the time we were herding our sheep near them." But Nabal didn't have it in him to even say a simple thank you. Such a fool!

Do you know what strikes me with greater force than these unflattering descriptions of Abigail's husband? It is her response. She quickly made plans to save his life. She planned to go and intercept the 400 fighting men bent on utter destruction. She knew that David was a skilled fighter. Everyone in Israel knew that; his exploits were the stuff of legion. But she also knew that Nabal was a wealthy rancher, not a warrior. It would be no match. Certain death was only hours away. Listen to verses 18-19: "Abigail lost no time. She took two hundred loaves of bread, two skins of wine, five dressed sheep, five seahs of roasted grain, a hundred cakes of raisins and two hundred cakes of pressed figs, and loaded them on donkeys. Then she told her servants, 'Go on ahead; I'll follow you.' But she did not tell her husband Nabal." She was wise enough to send the food originally asked for by David. The nourishment would at least temporarily detain the hoard from its advancement. And who knew, maybe once they had a good meal in their bellies they'd be willing to negotiate. Only time would tell.

Don't you think Abigail could have taken such private information from the servant and escaped, glad someone else was finally going to do what she'd thought about for years—kill the beast? She could have taken a quick trip to her mother's and returned after the dust settled. No, not Abigail. Remember wisdom is the acquired ability to live life well. Even if Nabal was a fool of a man, that was no reason to stand idly by while a death plot was forming against him.

Solomon, who wrote the Proverbs, wasn't even born yet, but his description of a wise woman fits our Abigail to a T. "The wise woman builds her house, but with her own hands the foolish one tears hers down" (Proverbs 14:1). Abigail built up when she had every reason to tear down.

These are still the two paths we can take in marriage today. We can be a builder or a destroyer. The choice is ours. We may live with a Nabal-like man or woman, with a great temptation to rip and destroy. She was too smart to take the easy way out. No wonder she is qualified to lead the way down the Avenue to Wisdom.

- ***Reflect for a moment on your marriage or even on your parents' marriage.***

- *Recall if there were more times of building or more times of destroying.*

- *Recommit to do things differently if you are married or want to be. If there is trouble, find someone to help . . . a trusted couple, a pastor or a trained marriage counselor.*

But if you think this was the only problem in Abigail's life, you are wrong. Problem number two was David himself. He was mad as he could be at Nabal and his foolish response. He was now determined to annihilate his whole family. This is how David expressed his thoughts to Abigail in verses 20-23: "As she came riding her donkey into a mountain ravine, there were David and his men descending toward her, and she met them. David had just said, 'It's been useless—all my watching over this fellow's property in the desert so that nothing of his was missing. He has paid me back evil for good. May God deal with David, be it ever so severely, if by morning I leave alive one male of all who belong to him!'"

Here usually-godly David allowed anger and revenge to rule the day. There was no indication that he prayed and asked God how to respond, as was his habit. We see no humility, patience or wisdom on David's part. We know he was accustomed to responding to provocation in an appropriate way. For example, in the previous chapter we read of an incident in which David exercised patience and wisdom in a hard situation. Saul was still the acting king of Israel but David was the chosen king. Saul, paranoid and fearful of David, had been chasing him around the region of Judah for some 16 years. In 1 Samuel 24, David at last had a perfect opportunity to kill Saul, yet he chose not to because it was not God's way. He controlled himself and acted wisely. Had David looked to God similarly in chapter 25, as he'd done in his ongoing conflict with King Saul, this whole mess with Nabal would have been averted. But no such restraint is evidenced in the chapter 25 encounter. David stepped off the Avenue to Wisdom and traveled the pathway of a fool.

God had some important lessons to teach David. He was actually using Nabal in David's life to reveal a side of David we'd not seen previously in the biblical record: The man had a temper. The man was capable of usurping God's control and acting out in his own power. These flaws needed to be surfaced and dealt with if he were to be a great king. God would use the negative experiences as well as the positive ones to teach this "man after God's own heart" how to trust Him.

- *Reflect on how God has used negative circumstances in your life to teach you more about Him.*

Again, Abigail's response amazes me. Did you notice how she just rode her donkey into the ravine? It is hard to overstate the amount of courage such an act would take. She was alone *and* she was married to the man who had angered David to begin with. This was perhaps the most dangerous moment of her life.

Abigail had her hands full of problems and so do we. It's easy to sail down the Avenue of Wisdom when all is right in the world. The trouble comes when things go a way we never expected and we have to make a choice to obey or disobey God, to act wisely or behave like a fool. Abigail stands as a stellar example of one who swallowed hard and did what was wise and prudent, not just in one circumstance, but as a way of life. She must have forgiven Nabal years before or she would never have responded the way she did in this time of crisis. This is further evidence of her strong walk with the Lord. Proverbs 1:7 states it best, "The fear of the LORD is the beginning of knowledge, but fools despise wisdom and discipline."

- *Think about the problems you're facing today.*
- *Pray and ask God how He'd have you respond.*

Avenue to
Wisdom

Following Him

When I Can't See
the End of the Road

135

Francois Fenelon, a French pastor from the 16th century, wrote extensively on developing a deep love for God regardless of the present troubles. His suggestions in the following excerpt from a letter to his parishioners still give timely advice for us who, like Abigail, want to love God in all circumstances.

> Tell God all that is within your heart as one unloads one's heart to a dear friend. Tell Him your troubles that He many comfort you, tell Him your joys that He may sober them, tell Him your longings that He many purify them, tell Him your mislikenings that He may help you to conquer them, talk to Him of your temptations that He may shield you from them.

> Show Him all the wounds of your heart that He may heal them. Lay bear to Him your indifference to good, your depraved taste for evil, your instabilities. Because if you pour out to Him all your weaknesses, needs and troubles, there will be no lack of what to say—you will never exhaust this subject because people who have no secrets from each other do not weigh their words because there is nothing to be kept back.

There is no other way to experience the reality of God amidst problems. If we are not being honest with Him about what we are feeling—the dark and the light side—problems will move us away from God. When we are praying about everything, God

will show us what to do, how to act and what to avoid. As we
read His Word we learn His will, His heart and what brings Him
pleasure. It is the wise man or woman who then practices what's
been read. Abigail did just that.

- ***Take time right now to do as Fenelon suggests.***

- ***Unpack all the issues that unsettle your soul.***

- ***Tell God you want to go deeper in your prayer life.***

HER PLAN

Because Abigail was free from a bitter, retaliatory spirit, she was
able to think and respond with wisdom, clarity and efficiency
when she heard David was headed her way. Her plan was simple:
she would act and speak wisely. Let's take a closer look at her
actions when the servant told her of David's plans. First, she
listened carefully. She was not quick to overreact or give in to
anger and impatience toward David or her husband. Her second
response was to send food and drink ahead of her coming, which
was exactly what David's men had originally requested. Thirdly,
she went to David personally to negotiate a peaceful solution.
This astonishing meeting is recorded in verses 23-31.

> When Abigail saw David, she quickly got off her donkey
> and bowed down before David with her face to the
> ground. She fell at his feet and said, "My lord, let the
> blame be on me alone. Please let your servant speak to
> you; hear what your servant has to say. May my lord
> pay no attention to that wicked man Nabal. He is just
> like his name—his name is Fool, and folly goes with
> him. But as for me, your servant, I did not see the men
> my master sent. Now since the Lord has kept you, my
> master, from bloodshed and from avenging yourself

with your own hands, as surely as the LORD lives and as you live, may your enemies and all who intend to harm my master be like Nabal. And let this gift, which your servant has brought to my master, be given to the men who follow you. Please forgive your servant's offense, for the Lord will certainly make a lasting dynasty for my master, because he fights the LORD's battles. Let no wrongdoing be found in you as long as you live. Even though someone is pursuing you to take your life, the life of my master will be bound securely in the bundle of the living by the LORD your God. But the lives of your enemies he will hurl away as from the pocket of a sling. When the Lord has done for my master every good thing he promised concerning him and has appointed him leader over Israel, my master will not have on his conscience the staggering burden of needless bloodshed or of having avenged himself. And when the LORD has brought my master success, remember your servant.

We learn so much about Abigail's character from her actions and her speech. Her confidence was in the Lord, and she was willing to risk her own life to save her husband and her household. I like what Jesus said about a person like her, "The good man [or woman] brings good things out of the good stored up in his heart, and the evil man brings evil things out of the evil stored up in his heart. For out of the overflow of his heart his mouth speaks" (Luke 6:45). And because Abigail's heart was pure, God could use her words as a vehicle to deliver David from sin.

I observe two major ways wisdom is seen in Abigail's verbal appeal to David. First, she was extraordinarily humble, as seen in the way she greeted David: She bowed down and fell at his feet. Did you count the number of times she addressed him as "my master" (seven) and "my lord" (two)? She called herself "your servant" six times and made direct references to the Lord another seven times. These are significant insights into her humble heart for God and her longing to find a way through this quagmire. She was even willing to take the blame for the whole incident (1 Samuel 25:24 and 28). The way of wisdom steers clear of the prideful response like Nabal's and David's because it makes matters worse. Wise people are humble people who want to work through problems and extend forgiveness. Humility is at the heart of what it is to be a believer. In the New Testament, in 1 Peter 5:5, we read, "God opposes the proud but gives grace to the humble." Jesus said He Himself was "gentle and humble in heart" (Matthew 11:29). I think Abigail's heart was much the same.

- *Identify any pride in your life.*

- *Consider how it manifests itself in your relationships.*

- *Ponder what James means by "God opposes the proud but gives grace to the humble."*

The second way I see Abigail demonstrate wisdom in her verbal appeal to David is in her truthfulness. She was truthful about the gravity of the offense were he to kill Nabal. It would be an ugly mark on his character and a heavy burden for his conscience. She came in gentleness and tact, to be sure, but she packed a punch when she reminded him that this was a foolish act to commit. Furthermore, she reminded him of his call to be king of Israel: "For the LORD will certainly make a lasting dynasty for my master" (v. 28). Her words were getting David's thinking back where it needed to be as the appointed leader over Israel (v. 30). Abigail's appeal was clear: Godly leaders do not behave like this. And lastly, she reminded him to keep his trust in the Lord who'd always been his protector and defender. This beautiful and intelligent woman came with a figurative cup of cold water and threw it in the face of David, encouraging him to wake up and look at this whole situation rationally and spiritually and not so emotionally. Seems that David had forgotten God—forgotten His love, care and provision. Perhaps that's why seven times in six verses Abigail used the name of the Lord to jumpstart David's memory.

She had a remarkable understanding of the breadth and depth of God's call on David's life, didn't she? She was aware of the conflict between David and Saul, aware that David would one day be king, and she had a great grasp on how God cares for His people. I love the fact that she knew the character and conduct of God and was able to speak of it in such an articulate and succinct manner.

- ***Reaffirm your desire to be a person who knows God in such a way.***

- ***Rethink what is involved in the process.***

Her plan was not elaborate, manipulative or seductive. She came with wise actions and wise words . . . words draped with humility and truth. I've got a few lessons to learn from the way Abigail approached problems with skill, intelligence and a bit of common sense. She was wise to steer clear of anger, panic and pride. Problems have a way of revealing our character, and Abigail's shone forth with godly brilliance. Unfortunately, the same problem highlighted new dimensions of Nabal's foolishness and David's anger. I want to learn how to trust the Lord in the middle of the problem and to respond as Abigail did. It is a major lesson I need to learn as I travel further down the Avenue to Wisdom. This is easier said than done. Too often the pressure of the problem brings forth impatience and anger. I am trying to take to heart James 1:19-20:

> My dear brothers, take note of this: Everyone should be quick to listen, slow to speak and slow to become angry, for man's anger does not bring about the righteous life that God desires.

- *Analyze the way you solve your problems.*

- *Think about what is exposed in your character
  when the pressure of problems hits.*

- *Ask the Lord to help you respond with humility
  and truth.*

Dr. Martin Luther King, Jr. had a godly character that stood the
test of trials, injustice and hatred, so I listen to his words:

> The ultimate measure of a man is not where he stands
> in moments of comfort and convenience, but where he
> stands in moments of challenge and controversy.

HER PRIZE

I love happy endings. When Abigail finished her plea to David
he said,

> "Praise be to the LORD, the God of Israel, who has sent
> you today to meet me. May you be blessed for your
> good judgment and for keeping me from bloodshed
> this day and from avenging myself with my own hands.
> Otherwise, as surely as the LORD, the God of Israel,
> lives, who has kept me from harming you, if you had
> not come quickly to meet me, not one male belonging
> to Nabal would have been left alive by daybreak." Then
> David accepted from her hand what she had brought
> him and said, "Go home in peace. I have heard your
> words and granted your request" (vv. 32-35)

I wonder if she expected such an immediate and positive
response? Although David had been conducting himself in a very
uncharacteristic manner, now we see the man after God's own heart.
As soon as he heard the truth, he changed his course of action. He

had been melted by Abigail's wise and penetrating words. I wonder if David had this incident in his mind when he penned Psalm 37:23-24? "If the LORD delights in a man's way, he makes his steps firm; though he stumble, he will not fall, for the LORD will uphold him with his hand." That is a hopeful thought for all of us because even godly people stumble. How good is God to lend us a hand when we do! Listen to the wise words of David Swartz:

> Often the hard way can be the very best way to make sure you never forget. Sin that's been confessed, wrestled with, and overcome is one of the finest teachers we have. Our struggles and defeats can increase our spiritual growth just as much as our victories—if we learn from them. . . . How can anyone grow through temptations, trials, and even the ravages of deep sin? We can all grow through the scars and brokenness because of the counsel, comfort, and healing of the God who uses all things—yes, even the desolate aftermath following sin—to bring us back to our spiritual senses and back to Him." *(Dancing with Broken Bones)*

- **Identify a time when you watched God take your mess and make something good from it.**

- **Pause and offer a silent prayer of heartfelt thanks for such amazing grace.**

I'll bet Abigail turned and headed for home with a spring in her step. She'd done God's will God's way, and now she received a joyous prize: Her household was saved and her king restored. The day turned out to be a good one after all. Now, granted, things didn't work out too well for Nabal. While his wife was out saving his life, he was throwing a huge, drunken brawl back at the ranch (I Samuel 25:36-38). He was so out of it when Abigail returned from her dangerous journey, she couldn't even tell him about her

Avenue to
Wisdom

Following Him

When I Can't See
the End of the Road

142

success. Wise people have a good sense of when things should be discussed and when they should not be. In sticky situations, timing is everything. By morning he sobered up, so she told him the whole story. He was so shocked or afraid—the text doesn't tell us why—his heart failed and he died ten days later. When the news reached David, he interpreted the events as God's just dealing with Nabal. And, apparently, Abigail's intelligence and beauty had not escaped his notice, because he asked her to be his wife. She gladly accepted. The ordeal ended in a way I am sure Abigail *never* anticipated. She would marry the future king of Israel! Only God could have had such a prize in mind for this wise woman of Carmel.

There are no guarantees for "happily ever after" endings for the problems in our lives . . . at least not now. Death, loss, grief, sickness, heartache, financial reversals, tragic mistakes and conflicts are a part of life. The Bible does not deny that reality. I haven't found a single character in the Bible who did not have problems. But what we can count on is a tearless, painless and joyful eternity . . . if we know the Lord. Listen to what Revelation 21:3-4 has to say about our future.

> And I heard a loud voice from the throne saying, "Now the dwelling of God is with men, and he will live with them. They will be his people, and God himself will be with them and be their God. He will wipe every tear from their eyes. There will be no more death or mourning or crying or pain, for the old order of things has passed away."

But for now we keep our feet firmly planted on the Avenue to Wisdom. Sure, there will be ongoing temptations to look out for. Shortcuts and occasional detours may even surprise us. But we shall not be detained or derailed. We are headed home and the way of wisdom is the surest route to our final destination.

Meditations for the Journey
WISDOM

Consider...

God's Word

> *The Lord gives wisdom, and from his mouth come knowledge and understanding.*
>
> **Proverbs 2:6**

> *The fear of the LORD teaches a man wisdom, and humility comes before honor.*
>
> **Proverbs 15:33**

God's Heart

> *My child, do not share thy burdens with all who come unto thee professing concern. Lo, I Myself am the great burden-bearer. Ye need not look to another. I will lead thee and guide thee in wisdom from above. All things shall be as I plan them, if ye allow Me the freedom to shape circumstances and lead thee to the right decisions.*

> **Frances J. Roberts, *Come Away, My Beloved***

144

Singing . . .

Be Still, My Soul

*Be still, my soul—the LORD is on thy side! Bear patiently
the cross of grief or pain; leave to thy God to order and
provide—in ev'ry change He faithful will remain. Be still,
my soul—thy best, thy heav'nly Friend, through thorny ways,
leads to a joyful end.*

*Be still, my soul—thy God doth undertake to guide the
future as He has the past; thy hope, thy confidence let
nothing shake. All now mysterious shall be bright at last.
Be still, my soul—the waves and winds still know His voice
who ruled them while He dwelt below.*

Katharina von Schlegel, 1697-1768

Praying . . .

*I have a hard time, LORD, trusting your wisdom because
I think I know what is best. I am slow to pray and slower
still to seek Your will and Word on the matter at hand.
Forgive me, LORD. I know that with You is all wisdom for
every situation. Remind me to turn to You quickly.* **Amen**

"The notion of God's love coming to us free of charge, no strings attached, seems to go against every instinct of humanity. The Buddhist eight-fold plan, the Hindu doctrine of karma, the Jewish covenant, and the Muslim code of law—each of these offers a way to earn approval. Only Christianity dares to make God's love unconditional."

Philip Yancy,
What's So Amazing About Grace?

Avenue to TRANSFORMATION

"Momma, do you ever thank God for good hair days?" asked my seven-year-old daughter. Having good hair was an important feature in her life at that time but even more significant that particular morning. It was "Spirit Week" at her school and one of the activities was to dress a different way each day. Monday was Red, White and Blue Day, Tuesday was Twin Day, Wednesday was Formal Day, Thursday was Nerd Day and Friday was School Colors Day. The problem was that I had misplaced the list that told me what outfit was to be worn each day. But I had guessed correctly for Monday and Tuesday so I figured I was on a roll. Wednesday *had* to be Formal Day. Much effort had already gone into looking just right for the big event. Brooke had laid out her clothes the night before in an anatomically correct manner at the foot of her bed; she'd gotten up early and now was upstairs waiting for me to finish her hair. Her final words as we piled into the car were, "Momma, I certainly look very beautiful today!"

Avenue to
Transformation

Following Him

When I Can't See
the End of the Road

146

But, when we reached school it became painfully obvious that it was *not* Formal Day but *Nerd* Day! We burst out laughing. I did an immediate U-turn and got home as fast as legally possible. In a matter of seconds Brooke went from looking her best to looking nerdy . . . crooked pigtails, baggy clothes and uneven socks. The transformation was immediate and amazing.

I love transformations. Some of my favorite magazine articles are the ones that show before-and-after pictures of a complete make-over. Many times it's hard to believe it is the same individual! It is incredible how a change in haircut and color, makeup and clothing can so alter a person's appearance. But it's even more awesome when a person's whole life is transformed not with hairspray and hot rollers but by following the God of the Bible.

Rahab was a most unlikely candidate for transformation. She was a woman who dressed in revealing clothing, wore too much makeup and hung around the bars. People whispered about her, avoided her like the plague and thanked God they were not like her. But she couldn't have cared less. She had a good business in the town of Jericho. Prostitutes always do well in a big city. At the moment we meet Rahab, she didn't know it, but her life was about to change dramatically. Two men were coming to her place on the wall of the city, but not for the usual reason. They were coming with a request and a promised reward that would alter her future in ways beyond her wildest imagination. In the Old Testament book of Joshua we get up close and personal with Rahab the prostitute. It is another wonderful story of God's grace and love toward one who, on the surface, seemed unlikely to receive either.

- *Recall a time when you were an unlikely recipient of God's attention.*

- *Think about how that made you feel.*

A LITTLE BACKGROUND

God had rescued His people, Israel, from slavery in Egypt and
led them across the desert. For 40 years He had faithfully fed
them and given them shelter, water and protection. Moses, the
man God used to humanly lead this great throng, had recently
died, and the mantle of leadership had been passed on to his
aide, Joshua. Now it was Joshua who was going to lead Israel into
the actual land God had promised this people for hundreds of
years. Their first major hurdle was Jericho, a well-fortified city
with walls up to 25 feet high and 20 feet thick. Joshua decided
to send in a couple of spies to scope out the enemy. They secretly
made their way to Rahab's place. After all, traveling men were a
common sight in her establishment. Their goal was to blend in,
get a glimpse of the land and return to camp with their report.
But things rarely go as planned. Word reached the king of Jericho
that spies were in town, and he sent guards to question Rahab on
their whereabouts.

HER ROTTEN REPUTATION

We've already learned a bit about our main character, but let's
delve deeper. The story of Rahab is found in Joshua 2 and 6.
Most every mention of her name is followed by the phrase, "the
harlot." Her reputation was a part of who she was. Both Christian
and Jewish commentators have tried to interpret this to mean
"innkeeper" or "bar maiden." It's simply too great a stretch
for them to believe that God could use a harlot to intervene on
behalf of His people and to then be a part of the Messianic line of
Christ. But God saw beyond the outward appearances to a heart
that was open to following Him, open to be changed in every way.
That tells us a great deal about the nature and character of God.
Rahab shakes up our categories. Some of you reading this cannot
believe that such a person would even be found in the Bible! But
God does use her in remarkable ways to show us that he is a God
of grace and forgiveness . . . the God of the second chance.

Avenue to
Transformation

Following Him

When I Can't See
the End of the Road

148

Glyn Evans says it well:

> God never gives up on ruin; in fact, He begins with
> ruin and works until He transforms them into things
> of beauty . . ... Ruined things are my defeat, but to God
> they are opportunities. When the earth was without
> form and void God sent His Spirit and His light to bring
> order out of chaos and beauty out of blackness. What He
> did physically for the original earth He does spiritually
> for people. It is a truth—there are no ruined people in
> God's category, only opportunities for God to display
> His creative power. There are no hopeless aspects of my
> personality, only aspects that are waiting to be touched
> by the power-driven fingers of God. *(Daily with the King)*

Rahab may seem like a hopeless case to us but not to God. She
carries the name "harlot" as a declaration throughout history
of God's peculiar and amazing grace. Is God's grace any less
peculiar and amazing in our lives and His forgiveness any less
miraculous? None of us deserves to be saved, forgiven and
adopted into the family of God. Our reputations may not be
as measurable and public as Rahab's, but each of us has been
separated from God because of our own sin. God cleansed us
the same way He did Rahab and turned our lives around just
as dramatically. Beginning our journey down the Avenue to
Transformation always starts with the assurance that we are
forgiven. If you are a follower of Jesus Christ, then the Bible tells
us you are fully forgiven, a brand new creature with a clean slate
before God. Talk about Good News! But sometimes we have
a hard time forgiving ourselves of sins committed. Memories
of past mistakes can replay in our minds and drain away the
freedom and joy God wants us to experience.

- *Thank God for forgiving you and wanting you to be His very own.*

- *Think through areas of your life that still need a touch from the Lord. Ask Him to do a fresh work of transformation.*

- *Consider Psalm 103:12 "As far as the east is from the west, so far has he removed our transgressions from us."*

A REAL RISK

Rahab took significant risks throughout this story. It's as if God gave her unusual boldness and insight well beyond her years and education. In Joshua 2, I count six risky acts which demonstrated her faith.

Risk #1 was when the king sent his guards to question her about the spies. This would have been an intimidating confrontation, to say the least—a town harlot questioned by the king's representatives. They demanded she bring the spies out at once. She calmly said that they had been there but had left some time ago, and then she sent the guards on a wild goose chase looking for the two men she'd actually hidden on her roof.

Risk #2 was that she hid the spies, the enemies of her people. It was an act of treason and would cost her her life if she were found out.

Risk #3 was when she deliberately put the king's men on the wrong trail. If they returned too quickly, went back to her house and found her talking to the spies, it'd be all over for her.

*Avenue to
Transformation*

Following Him

*When I Can't See
the End of the Road*

150

Risk #4 was that she wanted to leave her own people and be counted among the people of God. Now think about that for a moment. She wanted to leave all that was familiar—her culture, language and customs—and go to live with an entirely different people group. Why? Well, she had heard about their powerful God and wanted to know and follow Him. Listen to how Rahab put it: "I know that the LORD has given this land to you and that a great fear of you has fallen on us, so that all who live in this country are melting in fear because of you. We have heard how the LORD dried up the water of the Red Sea for you when you came out of Egypt, and what you did to Sihon and Og, the two kings of the Amorites east of the Jordan, whom you completely destroyed. When we heard of it, our hearts melted and everyone's courage failed because of you, for the LORD your God is God in heaven above and on the earth below. Now then, please swear to me by the LORD that you will show kindness to my family, because I have shown kindness to you. Give me a sure sign that you will spare the lives of my father and mother, my brothers and sisters, and all who belong to them, and that you will save us from death" (Joshua 2:9-13). Rahab did not know if the Israelites would even welcome her into their camp and she certainty couldn't imagine what the transition would feel like. But people of faith want to be counted with God's people. They are ready, willing and desirous to leave their old life behind in search of a new one with God.

Risk #5 was that she let the spies down by a rope from her window. As I mentioned, she lived on the wall of the city. This was not an uncommon place for a home in Joshua's day. But it was very dangerous for her to let the men crawl out of her window. If anyone saw this, she would have been implicated in the plot against her own people. This act, too, would have been fatal for her if discovered by the powers that be.

*Avenue to
Transformation*

Following Him

*When I Can't See
the End of the Road*

151

Risk #6 called Rahab to action even before she knew for certain that the spies would return. The men asked her to tie a scarlet cord from her window so they would know where to come and get her and her family when the battle began. A cord hanging from a window would have been a sign sure to be recognized by the king's guards who were already aware of the Israelites' advance. Plus, she still had to convince her family to gather in her home and wait for the rescue. Any member of her family could have turned her in to the authorities.

Rahab showed her significant transformation by these actions of faith. We do not have a clear indication of when she placed her trust in God, but it must have been before the spies even arrived, because once they showed up, we can see that Rahab truly believed by what she said and how she acted. A nonbeliever would never have risked her life over and over again for an invading foreign army. She truly believed that the God of Israel was powerful enough to save her, and He was real enough to her that she wanted to be one of His own.

Again quoting Glyn Evans,

> Biblical faith is looked upon as a spring of action,
> a spiritual activator, a lifted latch that allows God's
> blessing to come pouring down. I must not merely sing
> about faith, or glory in it, but I must do what my faith
> requires. The heroes of the Bible did not believe in
> belief; they accepted the consequences of commitment.
> *(Daily with the King)*

That is exactly what Rahab did; she clearly demonstrated her commitment to God with each risk she took. How active and practical is your faith? Have you taken any real risks lately? For many, just becoming a Christian involves real risk. We risk relationships with friends when we choose to follow the Lord.

Avenue to
Transformation

Following Him

When I Can't See
the End of the Road

152

We risk our relationship with family members when we make Jesus our Savior. When I became a Christian at the University of Oregon, many of my dorm mates formed a club called the "Heathens for the Eradication of Stupidity." They began writing letters to the editor in the university newspaper belittling the existence of God and anyone dumb enough to believe. These were the girls who put the signs on their dorm doors that read, "Have you heard the good news? Jesus Christ is dead." It was devastating to my young faith. They would have absolutely nothing to do with me. In that hostile environment it was risky to believe, but I was now a follower of God and nothing would turn me back. As I've studied the people in the Bible, I've noticed that one evidence of their authentic faith is the desire to distance themselves from their old life and be counted with God's people and God's ways. The disciples left the fishing business, Abraham left Ur, and Shadrach, Meshach and Abednego left the king's presence, refusing to do what Nebuchadnezzar demanded. Biblical faith chooses to stand on God's side regardless of the cost.

- *Recommit yourself to stand for God.*

- *Note some real risks you've taken for the Lord.*

Read the book of Acts and note the commitment of the early church. These people were chased out of town, imprisoned, flogged and killed for their faith. Now, most of us will never experience that level of persecution for our faith, but we will have some. When it happens (notice I say "when" not "if"), turn quickly to the Lord in prayer, tell Him how it hurts and allow Him to strengthen and encourage you. When I need a little perspective I head to James 1:12, "Blessed is the man who perseveres under trial, because when he has stood the test, he will receive the crown of life that God has promised to those who love him." God will actually use the trials, persecutions and hardships to conform us more perfectly to the lovely image of Jesus. Knowing that puts a whole new light on life's complications, doesn't it?

- *Apply the James passage to the trials in your life.*

- *Think about what bold step of faith God is encouraging you to take.*

- *Pinpoint what holds you back.*

Forward progress down the Avenue to Transformation is sustained by our willingness to take real risks of faith. It is always a little scary, but such boldness deepens our resolve to follow Him all the way to the end. Henry Blackaby sums up this point in his book *Created to Be God's Friend*.

> He [God] looks for a quality of relationship toward Him that will respond in faith! Faith, then, is a quality of response to God that is expressed in trust, reliance, commitment and obedience. It is an unquestioned obedience, based on who He is, and the person's experience of God as He is! Faith is based on what we know of God as He has made Himself known and as we have experienced Him. The more we simply respond to Him openly and confidently, the more He reveals of Himself. The more He reveals, the more we can trust and respond. Therefore, a growing faith is when God systematically reveals Himself and we believe Him and respond to Him.

Rahab was a responder to God. From our first introduction we see her unique belief and relationship with God. Her experience with God was limited but she acted on what she knew, and God continued to bless her faith responses.

*Avenue to
Transformation*

Following Him

*When I Can't See
the End of the Road*

154

A RADICAL RELATIONSHIP

We've come a long way in our peek into Rahab's life, but we still need further explanation as to why she did what she did. It cannot be overstated how consistently she risked her very life to help these two spies *before* she had any concrete evidence they'd hold up their end of the bargain. I think the only rationale behind her actions is her faith in God. I have already quoted her statement of belief to these two men. She did not know a whole lot about God but she clearly knew enough to risk her life and the lives of her loved ones. Rahab had somehow heard enough about the God of the Israelites to place her faith and trust in Him. I count four indicators of her radical relationship with God:

1. She had a grasp on both the power and purposes of God. She told the spies on the roof that evening, "I know that the LORD has given this land to you." She'd only heard reports but that was enough to convince this woman that God was with this people. She heard of all the miracles and knew that only the one true God could do such things.

2. She believed the Word of God. With the above statement, she demonstrated more faith than did many of the people of Israel. A whole generation of God's people had perished in the wilderness because they had *refused* to believe that God had given them the land. Forty years earlier the Lord had led them right up to the borders and given them the go-ahead to take the land, but because of fear and unbelief, they never did (only Caleb and Joshua believed God and were still alive at this time). Now it was their children who were with Joshua, doing what God had always wanted: possessing His Promised Land. But here was this harlot-turned-believer who knew this land was given by God. Pretty amazing.

3. When she heard about God, she responded in faith—and so could all of the people of Jericho. She spoke in plural terms when she related to the spies, "*We* have heard how the LORD dried up the waters of the Red Sea . . . *everyone's* courage failed because of you . . ." (Italics added.) But we are told in chapter 6 that the people of Jericho shut their city up as tight as a drum to keep the Israelites from coming in. It seems that everyone in that city heard the exact same things as Rahab, but she greeted the news with *belief* while the other people hid behind the walls of *unbelief.*

4. She acted on what she believed. Rahab opened not only her home to the spies but also her heart to their God. She said she knew that the Lord was God. That's all it takes to be a part of God's family, and she wanted to be a member.

Her new relationship with God changed everything about her life—her profession, her people and the place she would call home. Why? Because she had a real encounter with God, and when that happens everything in a life is altered. Granted, she had much to learn, but her faith was deep enough for her to act in sweeping manner and to risk her life.

Isn't the same true for us all these years later? Our knowledge of God should affect everything about us. God is now our Lord and Master so we want to do His will and not our own. Think of the many ways you act and think differently since you met the Lord and chose to follow Him. Whether we've known the Lord for many years or are just getting started, our understanding of the Lord will dictate our obedience. So we need to press on to know Him better and better. Our relationship with God is more than just fire insurance to keep us out of hell, more than a contractual arrangement to ensure we'll get into heaven. It is a relationship, a love relationship with the King of Kings and the Lord of Lords. Our walk with the Lord is described in the Bible in the most intimate ways possible: Father/daughter, Shepherd/sheep, Potter/

Avenue to
Transformation

Following Him

When I Can't See
the End of the Road

156

pot and Husband /wife. We are invited to abide in Him, pray to Him about everything. and look to Him for the supplying of our daily needs. Jesus said that we are to love Him supremely and follow wholeheartedly. This needs to be a moment-by-moment choice. It is easy to get a bit lazy and distracted by a host of other things in our world, isn't it? We need to learn to keep the Lord central *and* live our lives, raise our children, go to work and clean the house. For me it means I pray all the time in my heart and talk to Him about everything that's going on in my life. I want to learn how to be more consistent at this practice. A.W. Tozer's warning is sobering:

> I want to deliberately encourage this mighty longing after God. The lack of it has brought us to our present low estate. The stiff and wooden quality about our religious lives is a result of our lack of holy desire. Complacency is a deadly foe of all spiritual growth. Acute desire must be present or there will be no manifestation of Christ to His people. He waits to be wanted. Too bad that with many of us He waits so long, so very long, in vain. (*The Pursuit of God*)

Do you have such a longing for God? Is He waiting for you to confess complacency and seek Him with fresh zeal? A radical relationship with God is built in much the same way a relationship with a friend is developed . . . through spending time together, by communicating with one another and seeking to please the one you care about. Don't put these practices off any longer. Ask the Lord to help you begin or continue to go deeper still in your walk with Him. When we travel along the Avenue to Transformation, we will notice our love for God expanding and our longing for Him deepening.

- ***Rate your "holy longing" for God. High? Medium? Low?***

- *Determine to read a Psalm every day for a month.*

C. S. Lewis suggests an exercise I practice often:

> It comes the very moment you wake up each morning.
> All your wishes and hopes for the day rush at you like
> wild animals. And the first job each morning consists
> simply of shoving them all back; in listening to that
> other voice, taking that other point of view, letting
> that other larger, stronger, quieter life come flowing in.
> And so on, all day. Standing back from all your natural
> fussing and fretting; coming in out of the wind. We
> can only do it for moments at first. But from those
> moments the new sort of life will be spreading through
> our system: because now we are letting Him work at the
> right part of us. It is the difference between paint, which
> is merely laid on the surface, and a dye or stain which
> soaks right through. (quoted in *Devotional Classics*,
> edited by Richard Foster)

- *Begin this practice tomorrow morning.*

- *Continue for a week, and record the difference in
  your relationship with the Lord.*

A ROYAL REWARD

Rahab's story does not give a time line so we don't know how
long it was before the spies returned to get her and her family.
I wonder if her relatives were as quick to believe and respond as
she was? Nonetheless, they ended up at her house on the wall,
waiting with her, scarlet cord still hanging from her window.
The way the scene plays out has an interesting twist. If you
think the Israelites gathered up their troops and marched off to

*Avenue to
Transformation*

Following Him

*When I Can't See
the End of the Road*

158

Jericho to defeat the people and rescue our damsel in distress, you're sadly mistaken. The instructions God gave them would test the Israelites' faith and Rahab's faith and ultimately give all glory to Himself. This is how it unfolded. God told Joshua to gather seven priests and have them carry the ark of the covenant into battle. He also told them to blow trumpets, probably rams' horns, until they returned to camp. Soldiers would precede and follow the priests, armed for battle. Joshua instructed them to march around Jericho one time and then head back to camp. Do you have the picture in your mind? A battle-ready army, marching around a major city, and the only sound to be heard is that of shuffling feet and rams' horns. An odd way to conquer a city, yet all obeyed. For six days they went through this drill. What was Rahab thinking? "This is no way to capture this city! Where is the fighting? When will they climb the wall? I will *never* be saved by this group." Perhaps her family was heckling her as well. Who knows?

But on the seventh day things changed. God gave them their marching orders again, but on this day they were to circle the city seven times and shout out a victory cry the seventh time around. And guess what happened? Those 25-foot walls just fell down! Can you imagine the shocking sound of these huge walls falling to the ground? The debris, rocks and immense clouds of dust must have covered the city that was once so mighty. Nothing is said about how Rahab and her family *could* have survived such an attack since her house was ON the wall that just came crashing down. But God must have done a miracle and kept part of the wall standing or protected them as the wall collapsed. Because soon after the crashing of the walls, Joshua gave the orders for the spies to, "Go into the prostitute's house and bring her out and all who belong to her." Whatever did happen, Rahab and her loved ones were rescued from this devastating scene. A fitting reward for this faithful woman.

Avenue to
Transformation

Following Him

When I Can't See
the End of the Road

159

The whole family was relocated to a place outside the camp of the Israelites until they could be cleansed properly according to Jewish law. But Rahab would not stay on the outskirts of Jewish life. She actually married a Jewish man named Salmon (Matthew 1:5) and became the mother of Boaz. Now, are you ready for this? Rahab became the great, great, great grandmother of King David! She is in the Messianic line of Jesus Christ (Matthew 1:5)! She is also one of two women mentioned in the "hall of faith" chapter (Hebrews 11:31). "Get out of here!" some of you are thinking. "How could a Gentile harlot be linked to Jesus and be counted as one of the most faithful?" Actually, it's perfect. This is the kind of work only God can do as we venture down the Avenue to Transformation. It's not about who you *were* but who you are *becoming.* I love what the apostle Paul said about God's transformation in 2 Corinthians 5:17, "Therefore, if anyone is in Christ, he is a new creation; the old has gone, the new has come!" When we accept Jesus Christ as Savior, everything changes. We become brand new people. God sees us as completely forgiven, fully loved and accepted into His family.

How does this transformation happen? It is as we learn the truth of God's Word and then live it out. This isn't just *hard* to do, it is *impossible* to do on our own. That is why the Lord has given us his own Spirit to live inside of us (Romans 8). When we become followers of Jesus, the Spirit of God takes up residence in our lives and empowers us to live in a way that pleases the Lord. He brings God's Word to our mind (John 16:13), He counsels us (John 14:26), He leads us to truth (John 16:13), and convicts us of sin (John 16:8). And that is just the beginning of all His marvelous works in our lives.

In view of the ministry of the Holy Spirit in our lives, it's no wonder that the apostle Paul said: "Do not get drunk on wine . . . Instead, be filled with the Spirit" (Ephesians 5:18). To be filled with the Spirit is to surrender our wills to Jesus Christ.

To put Him at the center of our lives, guiding us in our decisions, leading us as we go our way through life and relationships. We are filled with the Spirit by confessing any known sin in our lives, experiencing God's love and forgiveness, and then *asking* Him to fill us with the Holy Spirit. This isn't necessarily an emotional experience, but it is a decision of the will to surrender to Him. We stay filled with the Spirit by keeping short accounts with God; that is, we are quick to confess sin as the Spirit brings it to mind.

- *Pause and ask the Lord if there is any unconfessed sin in your life.*

- *We are filled with the Spirit by faith. If you want to be filled, pray a prayer something like this: "Dear Father, I want to be filled with Your Spirit as You commanded me to be filled (Ephesians 5:18). I thank You that You answer prayers prayed according to Your will (1 John 5:14-15). I am tired of trying to live the Christian life in my own power. I confess this sin to You: _____. Thank You for forgiving me because of Christ's death on the cross. Take control of my life because I want You to be Lord of all of me."*

- *Go through this process each time you sin and just watch the difference it makes in your life.*

The Lord loves to lead us down the Avenue to Transformation. He is a God who is in the business of changing lives. The closer we follow the more He will change us, until one day we shall be like Jesus.

Meditations for the Journey
TRANSFORMATION

Consider . . .

God's Word

*Come, let us go up to the mountain of the LORD, to the
house of the God of Jacob. He will teach us his ways, so that
we may walk in his paths.*

Micah 4:2

*Do not fear, for I am with you; do not be dismayed, for I
am your God. I will strengthen you and help you; I will
uphold you with my righteous right hand.*

Isaiah 41:10

God's Heart

*Give me grace to be holy, kind, gentle, pure, peaceable,
to live for Thee and not for self, to copy Thy words, acts,
spirit, to be transformed into Thy likeness, to be consecrated
wholly to Thee, to live entirely to Thy glory.*

***Valley of Vision*, edited by Arthur Bennett**

*Meditations
for the Journey
Transformation*

Following Him

*When I Can't See
the End of the Road*

162

 *Singing* . . .

O For a Thousand Tongues

*O for a thousand tongues to sing my great Redeemer's praise, the
glories of my God and King, the triumphs of His grace.*

*My gracious Master and my God, assist me to proclaim, to
spread through all the earth abroad the honors of Thy name.*

*Jesus, the name that charms our fears, that bids our
sorrows cease, 'tis music in the sinner's ears; 'tis life and health
and peace.*

*Praise Him, ye deaf; His praise, ye dumb, your loosened
tongues employ; ye blind, behold your Savior come and leap, ye
lame, for joy.*

Charles Wesley, 1707-1788

 *Praying* . . .

*To praise You more and more, this is the great longing of
my heart, Lord. I agree with King David when he said that
You had lifted him up out of a slimy pit and put a new
song in his mouth, and that many would see this change
and place their trust in You. Oh, do that in my life! May I
be a clear witness of Your power to transform a life, lifting
it from the pits of sin to the heights of acceptance, into the
very family of God. Thanks and ever thanks.*

Avenue to COURAGE

Thousands of college students had gathered in a peaceful protest for democracy at Tiananmen Square in Beijing, China. The group had erected a figure vaguely resembling the Statue of Liberty called the "goddess of democracy." It became the rallying point and symbol of the freedom they sought. As their number grew, time seemed to add to their moral strength. The whole world was watching. Eventually, the government sent in the military to break up the protest. A courageous young man captured the imagination of the world when he single-handedly stopped the advance of a tank column by standing in its way. One slender college student dressed in dark slacks and a white shirt against tons of steel. Sadly, his resistance wouldn't hold off what was to come. The military opened fire on the students. Nearly 1,000 lost their lives, many others were arrested and the remainder fled back to their classrooms. That young man remains etched in my mind as such a symbol of reckless courage and selfless determination.

John Eldridge quotes G.K. Chesterton in his book *Wild at Heart* and captures the spirit of courage:

> "He who will lose his life, the same shall save it," is not a piece of mysticism for saints or heroes. It is a piece of everyday advice for sailors or mountaineers. It might be printed in an alpine guide or a drill book. The paradox is the whole principle of courage, even of quite earthly or quite brutal courage. A man cut off by the sea may save his life if he will risk it on the precipice. He can only get away from death by continually stepping within an inch of it. A soldier surrounded by enemies, if he is to cut his way out, needs to combine a strong desire for living with a strange carelessness about dying. He must not merely cling to life, for then he will be a coward, and will not escape. He must not merely wait for death, for then he will be a suicide, and will not escape. *He must seek his life with a spirit of furious indifference to it; he must desire life like water and yet drink death like wine.* (Italics added.)

Not everyone is given to bold and obvious displays of courage, but we all admire the quality. We are drawn to movies, novels and stories where the main characters demonstrate startling acts of courage. As a young girl, I couldn't read enough about Anne Frank, a Jewish girl who hid in an attic with her parents from the hideous rampage of Hilter's SS troops. She dared to dream about a future of freedom and wrote with extraordinary sensitivity about her feelings of entrapment. Courage embodied in a young teenager.

When I became a Christian in college, I was introduced to the writings of Corrie ten Boom. She lived about the same time as Anne Frank and was a strong follower of Jesus Christ. Her family hid Jewish people in their house and they were ultimately arrested and carted off to the concentration camps. Corrie lost her beloved father and sister in the camps and was finally released because of a clerical error. She spent the rest of her life traveling the globe, teaching on biblical forgiveness. Corrie emulated the same courageous spirit that our Lord Jesus demonstrated when he hung on the cross and said, "Father, forgive them, for they do not know what they are doing" (Luke 23:34). After her release from Ravensbruck, Corrie once came face to face with a member of the SS troops who'd guarded her. What she did next was astonishing: she forgave him. He burst into tears and eventually placed his faith in Christ. Courage embodied in a little old woman.

- ***Think of people you know who have demonstrated courage.***

- ***What can you learn from their example?***

Webster's Dictionary defines courage as "mental or moral strength to venture, persevere and withstand danger, fear or difficulties." Courage implies strength in overcoming fear and in persisting against the odds or difficulties. The Bible is full of people who withstood difficulties and not only persevered but were victorious. Jeremiah, John the Baptist, and the apostle Paul lived lives and preached messages that were controversial, and they paid a price for their courage. Each was imprisoned, several lost their lives, but not one changed his commitment.

There is a woman tucked away in the Old Testament who has pricked my interest and challenged my thinking about courage. She did not begin very courageously yet, through a string of events, found herself in a critical and crucial place where she *had* to overcome fear and persist amidst great obstacles. That's why she is a perfect guide down the Avenue to Courage. Queen Esther's story is found in the book that bears her name.

SETTING THE STAGE

Esther didn't plan on being an example of courage. She was just a young Jewish woman living in exile in Babylon with her adoptive father, Mordecai. Esther's parents had been killed, perhaps when the Jews were conquered by Nebuchadnezzar, then king of Babylon, and dragged off to his empire. All the Jews hated being away from their beloved Promised Land, but Mordecai and Esther had made the best of their circumstances. Mordecai was a royal official in the capital city of Susa and sat at the king's gate with the other nobles of the land.

Esther was a gorgeous young woman, a stand-out, really, for her beauty of form and feature. So when word reached the people of the land that the king was holding a contest to find the most beautiful virgin to be his new wife, Mordecai filled out an application for Esther. It seems the king's current wife, Vashti, had fallen out of favor because she refused to dance for him and his guests at a recent party. Although King Xerxes' anger eventually subsided, his decision to banish his former wife from his presence did not. The hunt was on for a new queen. Young virgins from throughout the country flocked to Susa in hopes of becoming the king's next wife. They were asked to undergo a year of beauty treatments before being presented to the king for his approval. This beauty regimen involved six months of treatments with the oil of myrrh and another six months with perfumes and cosmetics. That's the kind of spa I'd like to visit! But before Mordecai allowed Esther to enter the year of preparation, he instructed her not to reveal her nationality or family background. Esther had always done what her adoptive father asked; she kept her heritage to herself.

When Esther appeared before King Xerxes, he was smitten! He had already seen more than a few of the virgins, but none held a candle to Esther. He crowned her queen right on the spot and threw a huge banquet in her honor. He even proclaimed the day a national holiday and distributed gifts to all with royal liberality. For the moment, it was a fairy tale story come to life, but things were about to take a drastic turn that would challenge this young woman's courage.

THE CRISIS

Mordecai had been tracking Esther's progress during the year of preparation as he sat at the king's gate. He must have been elated when his own daughter was crowned queen, but that joy was sobered by a couple of significant events. The first was when he discovered a plot to kill the king, planned by fellow officials. As soon as all the facts were in, he told Esther, who in turn reported it to the king, and the two conspirators were hung on the gallows. The second event was far worse. It was a plot to kill Mordecai's people, the Jews.

Haman, another royal official, had recently been promoted by the king to the office of chief noble. He soon demanded that all the other officials bow down to him every time he showed up in the court. Mordecai was a godly Jew who bowed down to God alone, so he refused to prostrate himself before the chief noble. Such insubordination infuriated Haman so much that he determined to kill the whole Jewish race! Obviously, Haman must have harbored intense hatred for the Jews to react with such violence and resolve. He made an appointment with Xerxes and told him his desires in very vague terms. He said that there

Avenue to
Courage

Following Him

When I Can't See
the End of the Road

168

were "a certain people" dispersed throughout the land who were disobedient to the king's wishes. He suggested it would be in the king's best interest to destroy them. Haman received approval to carry out this atrocity. A royal proclamation was issued in all the languages of the provinces announcing the plan to annihilate all Jews—men, women and children—on the 13th day of the month of Adar (February-March), about 11 months away. Naturally, when Mordecai heard about the plot, he was devastated, as were the rest of the Jews throughout the kingdom. One way Jewish people expressed their grief at this time was to tear their clothes and put ashes on their heads. So Mordecai sat outside the palace and did both. We can only imagine the utter shock and disbelief such news would bring as the Jews envisioned the murder of their children and themselves, their entire race destroyed.

Word of Mordecai's immense grief reached Esther, who had not yet heard of the brutal plan. Worried, she sent him a fresh set of clothes, but he refused to be comforted and sent the outfit back to the queen. Esther continued to try to reach her father and find out what was troubling him. She sent one of her servants to get the whole story, and Mordecai relayed the tragic turn of events. The conversation ended with his desperate appeal to Esther to go to the king to beg for mercy and plead for the life of her people. Esther's first response did not have a courageous ring to it, "All the king's officials and the people of the royal provinces know that for any man or woman who approaches the king in the inner court without being summoned, the king has but one law: that he be put to death. The only exception to this is for the king to extend the gold scepter to him and spare his life. But thirty days have passed since I was called to go to the king" (v. 4:11). That was her reply. It was a polite "thanks, but no thanks." It seems she figured it was a bit too risky to go uninvited into the king's court, and maybe she even hoped Mordecai had another plan.

Avenue to
Courage

Following Him

When I Can't See
the End of the Road

169

But there was no other plan. This was a crisis of monumental proportion. Their people were about to be annihilated, and Esther was in a position to at least try to help.

Mordecai did not take "no" for an answer. He sent back a final appeal to persuade her to act. "Do not think that because you are in the king's house you alone of all the Jews will escape" (v. 4:13). He was not going to let her off the hook. He reminded her of her heritage. She was a Jew and would not escape death. Granted, he'd advised her to keep that to herself, but things had radically changed. *Her* neck was on the line as well. Had she forgotten she was a Jew? Maybe she thought she would have special protection as the queen. Her reasoning is unclear, but Mordecai's resolve is not. He was determined to personalize the problem and get her to change her mind: "Do you think *you'll* escape?" Of course she would not elude death. All Jews would die. Mordecai just wanted her to do the right thing and go in to the king. It would call for her to lay her life on the line for her people, but death was imminent no matter what she decided.

- *Recall a personal crisis you've experienced.*

- *Note what was required of you to persevere.*

THE CHALLENGE

Jim Elliot, the martyred missionary, once said, "Most Christians wait for a supernatural call from God to serve Him. What most need is a good, swift kick in the pants!" (Source unknown.) Mordecai was going to provide just that to his dear Esther as he continued to press his appeal, "For if you remain silent at this time, relief and deliverance for the Jews will arise from another place, but you and your father's family will perish. And who knows but that you have come to royal position for such a time as this" (v. 4:14)?

Avenue to
Courage

Following Him

When I Can't See
the End of the Road

170

Mordecai challenged her in two ways. First, he urged her to be a part of God's great plan of deliverance for His people. Mordecai was demonstrating extraordinary faith in God. Even though the most powerful people on earth had decided to take the Jews out, he was quite assured the plan would not succeed. Esther could be part of the problem or part of the solution. Even though God's name is never mentioned in the book of Esther, His fingerprints are all over this story of faith and deliverance. Secondly, Mordecai challenged her to use her position as queen to gain access to the king and rescue her people. Mordecai was asking her to see the hand of God in her selection as queen so that she would act at "such a time as this." It was no accident, no fluke of nature, that she had been chosen out of all the virgins in the land. This edict was a horrible tragedy, but the sovereign God was not caught unaware. Mordecai reminded her that God would use another if need be, but His clear desire was that she be the woman of the hour.

Dealing with crises and facing challenges are not limited to Queen Esther. Each of us is called to live courageously and act for God in the places He has put us. Several principles can be identified from this story to help us do just that. First, we must realize that God is sovereign. We follow Him no matter what. Even when things seem like they have taken a bizarre turn, we can trust Him. We need to remember that He places us in the roles we fill, the neighborhoods we live in and the relationships we enjoy or even struggle with. You may be blessed with great wealth, influence, opportunities or expertise; all of these things come from His hand, and we have the joy of being used by Him in these places He has put us. This principle took on new meaning for me a year ago.

I was flying home from New York, exhausted from a weekend of ministry. I just wanted to stare out the window. While I was waiting to board the plane, I saw a gentleman at the back of the line and just knew I'd be talking to him about the Lord. I was in the window seat with the middle one empty—until just moments before the airplane door closed. Guess who was walking down the aisle to take the last available seat? You're right, the man from the ticketing area. I did not *feel* like talking to him or to anybody else for that matter, but I knew the Lord had sovereignly arranged for this meeting and He wanted me to follow His leading.

So I began asking questions. "Where have you been? Where are you headed? What do you do for a living?" Typical I-hope-to-talk-with-you-about-Christ questions. And the conversation did turn that way. He was a college professor returning from a wild time at Mardi Gras. He asked me where I'd been, and when I told him I'd been speaking for a Christian women's conference, I could tell he was a bit less interested in continuing the conversation. He had some bones to pick with various Christian ministries he felt were hateful. When he told me he was gay, I understood his comments better. He was surprised to learn that I helped to start a ministry in Minneapolis that put together Christmas baskets for people living with HIV or AIDS. He was shocked because he assumed all Christians hated gays and wanted them to go to hell. I shared my testimony about becoming a follower of Jesus and told him about the unconditional love of God. He did not come to faith, as far as I know, but he left with a fresh desire to read the Bible and consider anew what it is to follow the Lord. Retrospectively, I am thrilled that I trusted God, who had a divine appointment for me even though it did not feel convenient.

Secondly, we must view ourselves as God's representatives and stewards of the possessions and opportunities He brings our way. Esther was the person whom God had ordained to be in the right place at the right time "for such a time as this." It would require extraordinary courage, to be sure, but she would not be alone as she ventured out. The God of Abraham, Isaac and Jacob would be with her. I wonder if she recalled the words of Moses to the Israelites just before they embarked on a new adventure against fierce enemies, "Be strong and courageous. Do not be afraid or terrified because of them, for the LORD your God goes with you; he will never leave you nor forsake you" (Deuteronomy 31:5-6). We, too, need to be reminded of that truth. God is with us, helping us to be brave when everything within us wants to shrink back.

- *Fill in the blank. "God has me _____ for such a time as this."*

The New Testament book of 2 Corinthians tells us that we are Christ's ambassadors, commissioned to tell others about His saving love. Like Esther, we must make the choice to trust Him and be courageous. We can share our faith, bring a meal, mow a yard or help that young missionary get out to the field. You don't have to be a beautiful queen to make a difference!

- *Review the unique places God has put you.*

- *Consider ways to be His ambassador.*

THE COMMITMENT

Mordecai's first request of Esther fell flat. Fear won out over courage, personal safety over personal sacrifice. But with his second request, he was making sense. God, behind the scenes, was at work in Esther's mind and heart. She was ready to make a commitment that quite literally could cost her her life. Now we see another side of this beauty as she readied herself to face this challenge with courage and strong resolve. Listen to her second reply to her father, "Go, gather together all the Jews who are in Susa, and fast for me. Do not eat or drink for three days, night or day. I and my maids will fast as you do. When this is done, I will go to the king, even though it is against the law. And if I perish, I perish" (v. 4:16). Faith won out over fear. She had clearly counted the cost of her actions and was ready to prepare spiritually for the task. Again, God's name is not mentioned, but she knew God had to intervene or all would be lost. That's why she asked all the Jews to stand with her in prayer and fasting before she ventured out. Esther was aware that it did not all depend on her. She needed God to work and others to pray. She was well on her way down the Avenue to Courage with these commitments.

- *Evaluate your spiritual fitness for the tasks in your life.*

- *Determine to have prayer be a part of every decision you make.*

- *Ask your good friends to stand with you when you are endeavoring to act courageously for the Lord.*

On the third day Esther prepared to enter the king's presence, looking her absolute best. She had prepared spiritually; now she needed to be prepared physically. I wonder if she had butterflies in her stomach as she dressed? Would today be the day of her

*Avenue to
Courage*

Following Him

*When I Can't See
the End of the Road*

174

funeral or the day she'd receive an invitation into the king's presence? Only time would tell. She made her entrance into the court, the king noticed her waiting, and without a moment's hesitation, he extended the golden scepter. The king immediately asked her what request he could fulfill on her behalf, up to half of his kingdom. She really must have been looking great! And with that, her life was saved; but much more needed to be done to ensure her people would be saved as well.

Her plan was profound and well thought through, as we shall see. Esther invited both the king and Haman to her place for a banquet that very day, and they accepted. Once they had eaten, Xerxes asked again what she wanted from him. She wanted them both to return tomorrow for another banquet! Haman left her house feeling like the second most popular man in the land. Happy and in high spirits, he went home and bragged to all his friends and family about these exclusive invitations to the queen's residence as evidence of his importance. Haman's arrogance and pride, already considerable, grew even more. But at the end of his little family gathering he remembered Mordecai, the man who refused to bow down to him, and Haman's joy turned to anger. His racially motivated complaint? "But all this gives me no satisfaction as long as I see that Jew Mordecai sitting at the king's gate" (v. 5:13). At his wife's suggestion, Haman built a gallows, 75 feet high, to hang Mordecai on the next day. Delighted, he awaited the morning. But God is greater than the hatred and bitterness of foolish people and was already at work.

It so *happened* that the king was unable to sleep that night and decided to review the history of his reign, discovering Mordecai's role in averting the king's assassination. Immediately, he resolved to reward Mordecai for this noble act—a rather timely decision, since Haman had planned Mordecai's execution for the very next day. How sovereign is God! He had been working quietly behind the scenes so far, but no longer. From here on out there would be a complete change in direction. Haman came before the king the next morning seeking permission to hang Mordecai from the gallows he had just built, but before he could make his request, the king asked him a question, "What should be done for the man the king delights to honor?" Now, of course Haman thought the king was referring to *him*, not Mordecai, so he answered in pompous detail: he should be given the king's royal crest for his head and royal robes for his clothes and then be led through the city streets on the king's horse while a servant announced to all, "This is what is done for the man the king delights to honor." Imagine Haman's horror when the king told him to do all this . . . for Mordecai! God was honoring his faithful servant at the hand of his mortal enemy (Proverbs 16:7).

Well, just as Haman finished leading Mordecai around town, it was time to go to Esther's for banquet number two. This time when the king asked for her request, she implored him to "spare my people." She reviewed the plot to kill the Israelites, and Xerxes, outraged, demanded to know the name of the man who had dared to plan such a thing. She revealed that it was evil Haman. The king was so incensed that he had Haman hung on the very gallows he'd built to kill Mordecai.

With Haman gone there was one more job for Esther, and that was to overturn the plan of Haman to exterminate her people. Again she appeared uninvited before the king, and again the golden scepter was extended and her request granted. This courageous young woman had done what she'd planned, and she had accomplished what she'd prayed. But much more happened than she could ever have expected:

- The king gave all of Haman's vast wealth to Esther;

- The *enemies* of the Jews were killed on the 13th day of Adar, the exact day Haman had planned to kill off the entire nation of Israel;

- Many non-Jews turned to the one true God because they observed His power to protect His people;

- Her act of courage was celebrated—and is still celebrated today—during the feast of Purim. The name is derived from the word *pur*, a Babylonian word for the lot used to decide when the Jews were to be killed. The festival name is a reminder to this day of how God intervenes on behalf of His people, no matter the circumstances.

- ***List some instances when God has done much more than you ever expected.***

- ***Pray through Ephesians 3:20 "Now to him who is able to do immeasurably more than all we ask or imagine, according to his power that is at work within us . . . "***

Three reminders rise to the top of Esther's story and serve as signposts on the Avenue to Courage. First, being a person of courage means we die to self and live for God. Paul speaks of how he did this in his own life. "Whatever was to my profit I now consider loss for the sake of Christ. What is more, I consider everything a loss compared to the surpassing greatness of knowing Christ Jesus my Lord, for whose sake I have lost all things. I consider them rubbish, that I may gain Christ and be found in him" (Philippians 3:7-9). Secondly, being a person of courage means we represent God boldly and honorably in the places He puts us. Listen to how the apostle Paul admonishes his disciple, Timothy. "So you must never be ashamed to tell others about our Lord. And don't be ashamed of me, either, even though I'm in prison for Christ" 2 Timothy 1:8 NLT. Paul also describes what faith looks like in Romans 4:18-21, "Against all hope, Abraham in hope believed and so became the father of many nations, just as it had been said to him, "So shall your offspring be." Without weakening in his faith, he faced the fact that his body was as good as dead—since he was about a hundred years old—and that Sarah's womb was also dead. Yet he did not waver through unbelief regarding the promise of God, but was strengthened in his faith and gave glory to God, being fully persuaded that God had power to do what he had promised."

- *Personally apply each of these reminders:*

  - *Die to self and live for God.*
  - *Be God's representative wherever you go.*
  - *Live by faith and not by sight.*

Jerry Bridges has a prayer I have written in my journal that encapsulates our study:

Lord, I am willing

To receive what You give,

To lack what You withhold,

To relinquish what You take,

To suffer what You inflict,

To be what You require.

(*The Dicipline of Grace*)

Avenue to
Courage

Following Him

When I Can't See
the End of the Road

178

- *Pray the prayer back to the Lord with all sincerity.*

- *Consider if you are willing to do what is suggested.*

Avenue to Courage: The name suggests it will take guts and gumption to get on and stay on this path. But it's not up to us to muster up our resolve and double our efforts; it's up to God. So don't go it alone. Take your heavenly Father by the hand, and He will lead you to the desired end.

Meditations for the Journey
COURAGE

Consider . . .

God's Word

*The LORD is my light and my salvation—whom shall I
fear? The LORD is the stronghold of my life—of whom shall
I be afraid?*

Psalm 27:1

*Give us aid against the enemy, for the help of man is
worthless. With God we will gain the victory, and he will
trample down our enemies.*

Psalm 108:12-13

God's Heart

*Be not afraid. I will not allow thine adversaries to swallow
thee up. Thou art My child, I shall deliver thee and honor
thee and I shall be glorified through thee . . . . Study My
Word, the Bible. Lo, it aboundeth with nuggets of courage.
They will strengthen thee and help thee, and even in
eternity ye shall partake of their far-reaching effects.*

Frances J. Roberts, *Come Away, My Beloved*

180

Singing . . .

Turn Your Eyes Upon Jesus

*O soul, are you weary and troubled? No light in the darkness
you see? There's a light for a look at the Savior, and life more
abundant and free!*

*His Word shall not fail you—He promised; believe Him, and
all will be well. Then go to a world that is dying, His perfect
salvation to tell!*

*Chorus: Turn your eyes upon Jesus; look full in His wonderful
face, and the things of earth will grow strangely dim in the light
of His glory and grace.*

Helen Lemmel, 1864-1961

Praying . . .

*I am not very brave, Lord. I fear rejection, I cower at the
thought of suffering, and I loathe the notion that my life may
have troubles and turmoil. And since all are real possibilities,
I desperately need Your courage and strength to walk in the
manner worthy of Your calling. Help me to believe that you
are with me wherever I go and that you will provide all I
need in every situation not only to endure but to be victorious.
Hallelujah!*

"The evil habit of seeking God 'and' effectively prevents us from finding God in full revelation. In the 'and' lies our great woe. If we omit the 'and' we shall soon find God, and in him we shall find that for which we have all our lives been secretly longing."

A.W. Tozer,
The Pursuit of God

Avenue to BLESSING

Who doesn't want to be blessed? We all have dreams of prosperity and enjoying happiness with our family and friends. Many think that a blessed life is almost synonymous with being an American, that is until we *live* life, and then we know that it is only a dream. Problems, perplexities and pain are far more a part of our daily realities than anyone told us when we were younger. Youth is mostly filled with fun and freedom. During the teen years and the 20's we are looking forward to all life will bring us . . . college graduation, the possibility of marriage and family, beginning our career and the opportunity of advancement, and the purchase of a home—all great things to look forward to. But for many, the 30's, 40's and beyond give us a healthy dose of reality. We discover that the families we were raised in were not very healthy, that our life doesn't fit the fairy tale we thought it would, and that there are far more difficulties than previously imagined. So now what? Give in to discouragement? Give up on our relationships? Or maybe gravitate toward cynicism?

- ***Raise your hand if this description fits a part of your reality.***

Jay Rathman understands that things don't always go as planned. He was deer hunting in the Tehema Wildlife Area near Red Bluff in northern California when he climbed toward a ledge on the steep, rocky slope of a mountain. As he reached the top he heard movement to the right of his face. A coiled rattlesnake lunged toward him, its bite just missing Jeff's right ear. His story appeared in *The LA Times:*

> The four-foot snake's fangs got snagged in the neck of Rathman's wool turtleneck sweater, and the force of the strike caused it to land on his left shoulder. It then coiled around his neck. He grabbed it behind the head with his left hand and could feel the warm venom running down the skin of his neck, the rattles making a furious racket. He fell backward and slid headfirst down the steep slope through the brush and lava rocks, his rifle and binoculars bouncing beside him.

> "As luck would have it," he said in describing the incident to a Department of Fish and Game official, "I ended up wedged between some rocks with my feet caught uphill from my head. I could barely move."

He got his right hand on his rifle and used it to disengage the fangs from his sweater, but the snake had enough leverage to strike again.

"He made about eight attempts and managed to hit me with his nose just below my eye about four times. I kept my face turned so he couldn't get a good angle with his fangs, but it was very close. This chap and I were eyeball to eyeball and I found out that snakes don't blink. He had fangs like darning needles . . . I had to choke him to death. It was the only way out. I was afraid that with the blood rushing to my head I might pass out."

When he tried to toss the dead snake aside, he couldn't let go—"I had to pry my fingers from its neck." (as quoted in *The Quest for Character* by Chuck Swindoll)

This is an incredible story with profound parallels to our lives. We can feel ambushed and attacked on almost a daily basis, can't we? Relationships sour unexpectedly, doctors' reports that indicate deeper problems blindside us, and our financial security can vanish without a trace. So can we *experience* blessing in the life we have? God in His Word answers the question with a clear and convincing YES. Why? Because He blesses us with *His* presence *in* the difficult places of life, thereby giving us hope and help to go on in joy. That's why we can stay on the Avenue to Blessing even when trials and troubles strike. Listen to a few of God's magnificent promises:

Even though I walk through the valley of the shadow of death, I will fear no evil, for you are with me; your rod and your staff, they comfort me.

Psalm 23:4

Avenue to
Blessing

Following Him

When I Can't See
the End of the Road

184

"For I know the plans I have for you," declares the
LORD, "plans to prosper you and not to harm you, plans
to give you hope and a future."

Jeremiah 29:11

[Jesus speaking] ". . . I am with you always, to the very
end of the age."

Matthew 28:20

For I am convinced that neither death nor life, neither
angels nor demons, neither the present nor the future,
nor any powers, neither height nor depth, nor anything
else in all creation, will be able to separate us from the
love of God that is in Christ Jesus our Lord.

Romans 8:38-39

- *Keep a list of promises from the Bible that*
  encourage you to keep on keeping on.

One of the reasons I love God's Word is that it tracks the lives
of people with problems. That surprises many who have never
read the Bible closely. For most Biblical characters, these issues
were very personal and hurtful. For example, Daniel, the Old
Testament prophet, was turned in to the authorities by his
contemporaries for praying and was tossed into the lions' den.
Joseph was thrown into prison on the false accusation of his
master's wife. Even the Lord Jesus was betrayed by one of His
disciples. But observing how these people fought the fight gives
us rich and vibrant examples of how to deal with the battles
before us today. The Old Testament tells of a woman in a very

lonely place, a place that many women today can relate to: She was infertile. And to make matters worse, her husband was married to another woman at the same time who *could* have children. This sad woman waged a brave battle on her knees and saw God do a miracle. The story of Hannah, found in 1 Samuel 1-2, reminds us that no situation is beyond God's supervision and that there is no reason why we can't stay moving on the Avenue to Blessing, even when burdens abound.

HER PERSONAL STORY

The story of Hannah occurred about 1120 B.C. Her family lived in Ramah, in the hill country about 15 miles north of Jerusalem. Hannah was married to Elkanah, who followed the custom of the day by marrying two women. Such a practice was never God's design but was a common choice of men in the Old Testament, especially if their first wife was barren. Elkanah's other wife was named Peninnah. The Bible simply records the facts without comment, "Peninnah had children, but Hannah had none" (1:2). Such a straightforward statement, yet behind those words are feelings of emptiness and extraordinary disappointment. "Infertile" is the last adjective a married woman wants attributed to her. It's one thing to *choose* not to have children; it's quite another when one *cannot* conceive. This was especially true in Hannah's day. A childless woman was considered a personal failure and an embarrassment to her husband.

Infertility is still a huge burden to bear for women who long to have their own children. Many of my friends have had to endure unkind words and false notions as to why they have remained childless. No one can understand the loss, no one can grasp the

*Avenue to
Blessing*

Following Him

*When I Can't See
the End of the Road*

186

sense of helplessness, and certainly no one can answer the "why" questions.

- ***If you are struggling with infertility, don't go it alone.***

- ***Find an older woman who has traveled the same road and talk with her about her journey.***

- ***Read books that deal with the issues of grace and godliness.***

- ***Keep pouring out your heart to the Lord.***

In Old Testament times the meaning of a name was especially significant. Hannah means "gracious; graciousness or favor." We will see that the way she treated the other wife and the way God treated her were indeed with grace and favor. Hannah was probably the original wife because she is mentioned first in the narrative. She may even have suggested her husband take another wife for the purpose of carrying on his name, in much the same way Sarah did for Abraham. What is clear is that Elkanah loved Hannah more than Peninnah. Twice in this short passage the text speaks of his love for her. This fact did not escape Peninnah's notice and she harassed Hannah "year after year."

This is not a happy beginning to our story, is it? Two wives (and you know that meant trouble!), wife number one was loved more but could have no children, and wife number two used her motherhood as a club. Now, this was a fun household to be in!

HER PROBLEM

*Avenue to
Blessing*

Following Him

*When I Can't See
the End of the Road*

187

Hannah's problem was two-fold. First, there was "the other woman" who lived under her same roof. The text identifies her as a rival.

> And because the LORD had closed her [Hannah's] womb, her rival kept provoking her in order to irritate her. This went on year after year. Whenever Hannah went up to the house of the LORD, her rival provoked her till she wept and would not eat (1 Samuel 1:6-7).

Peninnah had lots of sons and daughters (1 Samuel 1:4) but not the first love of her husband. She seemed to use that advantage to batter Hannah over the head, year after year. Hannah's problem with the second wife was a constant tension and there was no escape. I am intrigued by the different ways these two women dealt with difficulties. One lashed out with hateful, bitter words. It seems that Peninnah was motivated by envy and jealousy, two emotions bound to destroy her and others. Nothing good is said about her in the entire passage. On the other hand, Hannah wept honestly about the cruelty and went to the Lord to pour out her heart. Her problems pulled her toward God as her comforter, protector and help. Problems will either lead us into the heart and promises of God or detour us away.

- *Make a mental note of the pressing problems you're facing today.*

- *Answer the question, "Are they pulling me toward God or yanking me away?"*

Avenue to
Blessing

Following Him

When I Can't See
the End of the Road

188

Problem number two was her childlessness. You know Hannah had prayed. You know she'd talked with her husband about the heartache. I'll bet she'd even belittled herself, wondering what was wrong with her. Sleepless nights, angry conversations with the Lord and even hurtful comparisons with her rival were undoubtedly a part of the process. Godly people in the Bible struggled with "no" or "wait" answers from the Lord just like we do. There are hundreds of questions in the Psalms alone that attest to the conflict in the heart of the writer. The psalmists could not figure out where God was when difficulty came calling as an uninvited guest. Read just a few of the questions posed:

> How long, O LORD? Will you forget me forever? How long will you hide your face from me? How long must I wrestle with my thoughts and every day have sorrow in my heart?
>
> **Psalm 13:1-2**

> My God, my God, why have you forsaken me? Why are you so far from saving me, so far from the words of my groaning?
>
> **Psalm 22:1**

> Will the Lord reject forever? Will He never show His favor again? Has His unfailing love vanished forever? Has His promise failed for all time? Has God forgotten to be merciful? Has He in anger withheld His compassion?
>
> **Psalm 77:7-9**

• ***As you read through the Psalms, make note of every question.***

The character of Hannah and Peninnah showed in their responses to trouble, and so does ours. One lashed out and one looked up. How do you act when the vise of difficulties is tightening around your life? What do you do when you're ridiculed or belittled for something you have no control over? Do hurtful or confusing circumstances draw you to God or push you away? If we're honest, the answer is, "I've trusted God and I've not trusted God." Part of growing as a Christian is learning to remember God and choosing to talk to Him when the lights dim and we can't figure out what's going on. Brennan Manning puts it as only he can:

> When I get honest, I admit I am a bundle of paradoxes. I believe and I doubt, I hope and I get discouraged, I love and I hate, I feel bad about feeling good, I feel guilty about not feeling guilty. I am trusting and suspicious. I am honest and I still play games. Aristotle said I am a rational animal; I say I am an angel with an incredible capacity for beer. To live by grace means to acknowledge my whole life's story, the light side and the dark. In admitting my shadow side, I learn who I am and what God's grace means. As Thomas Merton put it, "A saint is not someone who is good but who experiences the goodness of God." *(Reflections of a Ragamuffin)*

- *Pinpoint your recent life pattern. Do difficulties cause you to lash out or look up?*

- *Think about steps that will help you remember God in your everyday life.*

HER PRAYER

Hannah was a woman of prayer. With just a few minor exceptions, the majority of her recorded words in these two chapters are her prayers or her comments on her prayers. Prayer is the way she dealt with the problems of her rival and her infertility. Our problems may or may not be like Hannah's, but we still have gobs to learn from her prayerful responses.

- *Call to mind a major issue you are facing right now.*

- *Note how prayer factored in Hannah's life, and consider if prayer would help you deal with the problem in mind.*

Remember that Peninnah was a constant source of ridicule. She provoked Hannah literally year after year until finally Hannah broke down and wept. At one point her husband saw how upset she was and asked her, "Hannah, why are you weeping? Why don't you eat? Why are you downhearted? Don't I mean more to you than ten sons?" It was his kind attempt to comfort her in the face of Peninnah's harassments. But she not only needed encouragement from her husband; she needed a good talk with God. So, while in Shiloh for a religious holiday, she went into the temple to pray, "O Lord Almighty, if you will only look upon your servant's misery and remember me, and not forget your servant but give her a son, then I will give him to the Lord for all the days of his life, and no razor will ever be used on his head" (1 Samuel 1:11). The writer of 1 Samuel gives insight into Hannah's emotional condition, "In bitterness of soul Hannah wept much and prayed to the Lord" (I Samuel 1:10). She was desperate for God.

The high priest, Eli, was present as she told the Lord all that
was on her heart. You'd think Eli would have been overjoyed
to see a godly woman so dedicated to the Lord and desirous of
doing whatever He wanted. Not this time. As if she'd not been
criticized enough by the second wife, she now got an earful from
Eli. He'd seen her moving her lips as she prayed and jumped to
a rather harsh conclusion, "How long will you keep on getting
drunk? Get rid of your wine" (1 Samuel 1:14). Whoa, talk
about a shot from left field! Hannah assured him that she'd not
been hitting the bottle but was a woman deeply troubled and
praying out of great anguish and grief. Thankfully, he believed
her and sent her away with his blessing and hope that God would
do as she'd requested. She left her problem with God and went
home with her family to Ramah, and guess what? She conceived
and bore a son, whom she named Samuel, meaning "because I
asked the LORD for him" (v. 20).

Wouldn't it be great if all our prayers were answered so perfectly?
I wish I could tell you that they will be . . . but it would not be
truthful. Why God seems to answer some of our prayers and
not others is wrapped up in the mystery of God's will and the
predominance of His sovereignty. We must choose to rest on His
unfailing love and His commitment to always do what is best for us.

Only when we follow God consistently will we have the resolve
to praise. This takes time and it takes maturity. A just-saved
saint and a seasoned saint will react differently to negative
circumstances and unanswered prayer. That's normal. But we
need to stay on a path of maturing by spending time with God
in His Word and prayer, by choosing to live in the power of the
Holy Spirit, and by keeping our lives free of sin.

- ***Make a mental list of unanswered prayers.***

Avenue to
Blessing

Following Him

When I Can't See
the End of the Road

192

- *Attempt to pray the commitment made by Job (Job 1:20-22).*

- *Ask God to help you still believe He can answer these prayers.*

Let's take some time and glean some lingering lessons from Hannah's prayer life and then make application to our own. I identify six insights for fruitful praying:

1. She knew where to go for help.

Hannah chose to go to the temple and pray, not sit around and have a pity party. She would go to the God who promises to be a very present help in our times of need (Psalm 46:1). Her husband loved her, but she had to go to God. The burden was too great for a human to handle. *Practical Pointer: Where do you go when the bottom falls out of your life? Do you settle for the help of people (best friend, spouse, family member) when God wants you to come to Him?*

2. She prayed specifically.

". . . [Do] not forget your servant but give her a son . . ." (1 Samuel 1:11). Hannah prayed specifically and God answered in like matter. Even if we don't see Him answer in exactly the way we've prayed, we are still developing an invaluable intimacy with Him each time we come to Him in prayer. *Practical Pointer: Start writing down each prayer request. Include the day you begin praying and the day you see God show up . . . even if He answers in a different way. It will be immensely encouraging to see how praying specifically encourages even more praying.*

3. She prayed persistently.

". . . she kept on praying . . ." (1 Samuel 1:12). This woman did not give up. How many years did she pray? How many times did she battle unbelief? Plenty, you can be sure. But she remained persistent. *Practical Pointer: Don't give up. My husband and I saw his 80-year-old mother come to Christ after 30 years of praying! Think through all the ways God has answered your prayers . . . health restored, a marriage or friendship mended, a wayward child returned home. There will be times when it's hard to believe, but be honest with God . . . He understands and wants to strengthen your resolve.*

4. Her prayer was from the heart.

Hannah was very honest with God. There was no attempt to sugar-coat her request or pretend spirituality. "I am a woman who is deeply troubled . . . I was pouring out my soul to the LORD" (1 Samuel 1:15). *Practical Pointer: How honest are you with God? Do you tell Him all that's going on in your heart? Journaling can be very helpful when you're learning to be honest. Often times we can write what is uncomfortable to speak.*

5. She demonstrated trust in God.

"Then she went her way and ate something, and her face was no longer downcast" (1 Samuel 1:18). I love this verse because it tells us that Hannah left her problem with God and believed He'd heard. There was no son, no answered prayer that she knew of yet; but her spirit was lifted simply because she had been with God. Prayer changes our perspective and gives us hope and peace, even before the answers come. *Practical Pointer: Go to*

Avenue to
Blessing

Following Him

When I Can't See
the End of the Road

194

God many times a day in prayer. Enjoy just being with Him and trusting Him for issues you cannot imagine how He will work out. Experience the pure joy of laying your burdens at His feet. You will be amazed what He will give you in return.

6. She gave God all the glory, praise and thanks for His answer.

First, Hannah did what she promised in her prayer . . . she dedicated her son, Samuel, fully to the Lord by taking him to Eli to be trained as a priest. Her words of dedication are moving:

"I prayed for this child, and the LORD has granted me what I asked of him. So now I give him to the LORD. For his whole life he will be given over to the LORD" (1 Samuel 1:27-28).

Little did she know that Samuel would become one of the greatest and most beloved priests of Israel. His mother was a woman who loved and trusted God, and he grew into a man who did the same.

Secondly, she prayed the most beautiful prayer of praise and thanksgiving to the Lord, recorded in the first ten verses of chapter two. She knew who was responsible for the birth of her son, and praise was the natural outcome of such an awesome answer. It's a prayer much like the one Mary, Jesus' mother, spoke when she learned she'd be the mother of Messiah (Luke 1:46-55). *Practical Pointer: When God answers your prayers, do you remember to thank Him with as much emotion as when you asked Him? Take a moment and write your own prayer of praise and thanksgiving for a recent answer to prayer. Make it a pattern, not an exception.*

Hannah was a genuine follower of God. Sure, there were times when she did not know where to go, how to pray or how to navigate through tough relationships, but she did not quit. Henry Blackaby explains the reason behind such a choice:

> When God "chooses" a person for His purposes, He does so according to the person's *heart!* The person must have a loyal heart full of trust and faith. God must have a person who loves Him "with all [the] heart, with all [the] soul, and with all [the] strength" (Deuteronomy 6:5; Matthew 22:37). Anything less than this is unacceptable to God for the carrying out of His purposes. Unless the person had such a heart, God would find the person arguing with God, rejecting God, disobeying God, and ultimately straying from God. The eternal purposes of God could not be accomplished in such a person's life. Only a *heart* that is thoroughly loyal to Him is acceptable to God. *(Created To Be God's Friend)*

- *Evaluate your heart's condition.*
- *Reflect on these descriptions from the Psalms and prayerfully apply them as God directs:*

  Upright in heart (11:2)

  A glad heart (16:9)

  A pure heart (24:4)

  A trusting heart (28:7)

  A broken and contrite heart (51:17)

  A stubborn heart (81:12)

  An undivided heart (86:11)

  A hardened heart (95:8)

*Avenue to
Blessing*

Following Him

*When I Can't See
the End of the Road*

196

A heart that goes astray (95:10)

A proud heart (101:5)

A dismayed heart (143:4)

Continuing down the Avenue to Blessing is an invitation extended to all whose hearts desire God's best. Hannah and many others of biblical and post-biblical times have left us clues as to how best to proceed. But the choice is ours to follow—even when we can't see the end of the road.

Meditations for the Journey
BLESSING

Consider . . .

God's Word

> *Blessed are they who keep his statutes and seek him with all their heart.*
>
> **Psalm 119:2**

> *Blessed are all who fear the* LORD, *who walk in his ways.*
>
> **Psalm 128:1**

God's Heart

Sometimes, Lord
You come up with such unpredictable answers—
Today
I related my predicament
I explained my desperation
I begged You
To get me out of this mess.
Your only answer:
"I beg you to let Me in on this mess."

Ruth Harms Calkin, *Tell Me Again, Lord, I Forget*

Meditations
for the Journey
Blessing

Following Him

When I Can't See
the End of the Road

198

Singing . . .

I Surrender All

All to Jesus I surrender, all to Him I freely give; I will ever love and trust Him, in His presence daily live.

All to Jesus I surrender, humbly at His feet I bow; worldly pleasures all forsaken, take me, Jesus, take me now.

All to Jesus I surrender; Lord, I give myself to Thee; fill me with Thy love and power; let Thy blessings fall on me.

Chorus: *I surrender all, I surrender all, all to Thee, my blessed Savior, I surrender all.*

Judson W. Van DeVenter, 1899-1993

Praying . . .

*The only way to obtain eternal blessing is to seek Your face, Holy Father. Seeking You means that there is **no one** and **no thing** above You. Forgive me, God, for seeking pleasures, revenge, financial security or a zillion other things over You. I repent of such idolatry. I agree with what the Lord Jesus said, "Seek first his kingdom and his righteousness, and all these things will be given to you as well" (Matthew 6:33). Grant me grace to obey out of love for You. **Amen.***

"Dear Lord, so far today I am doing all right. I have not gossiped, lost my temper, been greedy, grumpy, nasty, selfish or self-indulgent. I have not whined or complained, cursed or eaten chocolate. I have charged nothing on my credit card. But I will be getting out of bed in a minute and I think I will really need Your help then. Amen."

Author Unknown

Avenue to INTIMACY

Our son Bryan was a precocious two-year-old when he made the move to "the big boy bed." It was our custom to tuck him in with a story and prayers, then enjoy our evening together. Sitting on the couch with the lights down low, Bob and I were beginning to unwind from another full day. Then, from down the hall came the plea, "Open-da-door!" As I approached our son's bedroom, I could see his little fingers wiggling underneath the door. His head was pressed against the floor and his lips were squeezed between the rug and the door. He was trying desperately to be heard. "Open-da-door!" he begged. He could hear our voices and knew we had not gone to bed yet. Trying to be good parents, we decided to wait a few minutes before investigating the situation further. When I went to check on him later he was sound asleep, right on the other side of the door, his fingers still poking out from underneath. So like Bryan! He always wanted to be with us. The only thing in his way was the door.

There is someone who is calling to you to open the door. He's no two-year-old waiting to get out of his room; He's God and He wants deeper access to our lives. Throughout the Scriptures the message is unmistakably clear, and perhaps it is best summarized in Revelation 3:20, "Behold, I stand at the door and knock; if anyone hears and listens to and heeds My voice and opens the door, I will come in to him and will eat with him, and he [will eat] with Me" (AMPLIFIED BIBLE). From the creation of Adam and Eve to the sending of His very own son, Jesus, God has reached out to establish a relationship of love with us. I am sure God had been reaching out to me and knocking on the door to my life for many years, but it wasn't until I was a freshman in college that I opened that door and gave Him entry. But that's just the *beginning* of the relationship. I need to choose to cooperate with Him and consent to follow Him every minute of every day. This is the pathway to growth and maturity as a believer. We follow Him because we can't see the end of the road and we need a guide who loves us enough to lead us through the many potholes, seeming dead-ends and countless detours that exist along the way. Enjoy reading these verses that remind us of God's promised guidance:

Who, then, is the man that fears the LORD?
He will instruct him in the way chosen for
him.

Psalm 25:12

Since you are my rock and fortress, for the sake
of your name lead and guide me.

Psalm 31:3

This God is our God for ever and ever; he will
be our guide even to the end.

Psalm 48:14

Teach me to do your will, for you are my God;
may your good Spirit lead me on level ground.

Psalm 143:10

The LORD will guide you always; he will satisfy
your needs in a sun-scorched land and will
strengthen your frame. You will be like a well-
watered garden, like a spring whose waters
never fail.

Isaiah 58:11

- *Choose one of the previous verses that applies most*
  to your present circumstances.

- *Write it on a 3 x 5 card and carry it with you for*
  a week as a constant reminder of God's guiding
  presence.

I have presented a lot of information about the lives of
people recorded in God's Word, to allow you to see how the
unchangeable character of God is consistent throughout time.
The ten women I have presented provide unique insight into
what it means to truly follow Christ. None of the women knew
where the road would lead. "Their faith still speaks today . . . "
(Hebrews 11:3). I have not found one wonam in the gospels that
didn't respond in faith to Jesus.

We've traveled down many avenues to get us to this final chapter
which is intended to lead us straight into the heart of God. On
the Avenue to Intimacy we will learn how to experience fresh
encounters with the Lord and keep Him a vital part of all we
do. Our guide down the pathway involves a practice that is
core to experiencing intimacy with the Lord: prayer. Prayer
is simply talking with God. It does not have to be religious or

Avenue to
Intimacy

Following Him

When I Can't See
the End of the Road

202

complicated. We can pray as we walk, kneel, sit or stand. We can pray out loud or silently. We can pray alone, with our friends or in a huge auditorium filled with people. Bottom line: We can pray whenever and wherever and however we want. God is most concerned with the attitude of our heart . . . that it be humble, teachable and open to Him.

- *Consider your concept of prayer.*

- *Identify areas in your prayer life you'd like to see change.*

CULTIVATING INTIMACY

Prayer is a major way for us to get closer to God. This may strike some people as strange because prayer may have always felt formal, structured and rigid. For many, prayer is right up there with flossing your teeth, eating your vegetables or exercising. You may not *like* it, but it's *good* for you! Such a comparison could not be further from the truth. Prayer enhances and enriches our relationship with God because we communicate with Him and He communicates with us. Intimacy with the Father develops and He becomes a vital part of all we do. Listen to how *Random House Dictionary* defines intimate:

> A close, familiar, usually affectionate or loving personal relationship; a close association or detailed knowledge or deep understanding; the quality of being comfortable, warm or familiar.

Most of us long for a prayer life that could be characterized in such a manner. This kind of intimacy is cultivated through prayer. There are three New Testament words that give us clear direction on how intimacy with God can be cultivated through prayer: **come, cast** and **call**.

When we come to the Lord, we acknowledge our need for Him.
Listen to what the prophet Isaiah said long before Jesus was born:

> "Come, all you who are thirsty,
> come to the waters;
> and you who have no money,
> come, buy and eat!
> Come, buy wine and milk
> without money and without cost.
> Why spend money on what is not bread,
> and your labor on what does not satisfy?
> Listen, listen to me, and eat what is good,
> and your soul will delight in the richest of fare.
> Give ear and come to me;
> hear me, that your soul may live. (Isaiah 55:1-3b)

The Lord wants us to come into His presence just as we are:
hungry, thirsty and in need of soul refreshment. Isaiah said these
words centuries ago but the application is very contemporary.
Which one of us cannot easily relate to the condition described
in these verses? But in an age of self-sufficiency, self-love and
self-confidence, few of us want to admit our need. Bill Hybels, in
his book *Too Busy Not to Pray*, exposes this tendency:

> Prayer is an unnatural activity. From birth we have
> been learning the rules of self-reliance as we strain
> and struggle to achieve self-sufficiency. Prayer flies in
> the face of those deep-seated values. It is an assault on
> human autonomy, an indictment on independent living.
> To people in the fast lane, determined to make it on
> their own, prayer is an embarrassing interruption.

There are hundreds of voices suggesting how we should have our
needs met. Just count the number of times TV advertisements
promise to change your life if you just use their products. We

Avenue to
Intimacy

Following Him

When I Can't See
the End of the Road

204

can even find ourselves coming up with our own solutions, "If only I had a different job, or better children, a longer vacation, a new house, a new husband, or just a husband! If only I had an evening out or a good night's sleep, then all would be well with my soul; I would be refreshed and revived." But Jesus said the burdened, the tired, the worn out, the burned out and the stressed out need to come to *Him* because He understands their plight; He will help them through it.

> For we do not have a High Priest Who is unable to understand and sympathize and have a shared feeling with our weaknesses and infirmities and liability to the assaults of temptation, but One Who has been tempted in every respect as we are, yet without sinning. Let us then fearlessly and confidently and boldly draw near to the throne of grace (the throne of God's unmerited favor to us sinners), that we may receive mercy [for our failures] and find grace to help in good time for every need [appropriate help and well-timed help, coming just when we need it] (Hebrews 4:15-16 AMPLIFIED BIBLE).

Notice that the writer of Hebrews invites us to "draw near". . . not to get a lecture on all the ways we've disappointed God or to be criticized for a shoddy performance. Quite the contrary. He wants us to come and receive help and mercy *in* our time of need. It took a while for me to grasp the significance of such an invitation. When I was a little girl I had "good" clothes for special occasions . . . Thanksgiving, Christmas or Easter. Maybe you did too. I had good dresses, patent leather shoes and a good coat, so when I needed to look my best, I could. When I became a Christian I thought I had to put on my "good clothes," and put my best foot forward whenever I talked to Him. It never dawned on me that I could come to God just as I was, disheveled and out of sorts. My sense of intimacy with the Lord skyrocketed when

I began talking with Him about *everything* that was going on within me. Dressing up the problem, dealing with it on our own, or running to the myriad of alternatives offered in our time won't do. Our intimacy with God is built on a foundation of helplessness and real need.

> Your helplessness is your best prayer. It calls from your heart to the heart of God with greater effect than all your uttered pleas. He hears it from the very moment that you are seized with helplessness, and He becomes actively engaged at once in hearing and answering the prayer of your helplessness. (O. Hallesby, *Prayer*)

- **Acknowledge a place of helplessness.**

- **Pray a prayer of helplessness.**

First we **come** to Him with all our needs and then we are invited to **cast** our cares and ourselves onto the lap of our God. First Peter 5:7 tells us, "Casting the whole of your care [all your anxieties, all your worries, all your concerns, once and for all] on Him; for He cares for you affectionately and cares about you watchfully" (AMPLIFIED BIBLE).

I never cease to be amazed at this startling request. Did you hear what this verse is asking us to do, and why? GOD wants *US* to bring Him everything that concerns us because He loves us. Amazing. And when we obey and do exactly as He asks, intimacy is deepened. But for many of us this will be a whole new endeavor. We have become very comfortable in our prayer lives *not* really being honest with God about all the less-than-outstanding stuff in our lives. Many of us are uneasy praying in incomplete sentences. We like to be able to at least *suggest* a couple of ways the Lord could answer! But sometimes the problems at hand are too messy even to suggest possible solutions.

One day, my daughter Brooke came up from her room in haste, asking for a pair of scissors. It was all about knots, the knots in her shoelace that would not come out. A job needed to be done, and scissors would provide the only solution. She was quite convinced there would be no other way to remedy the situation. I said, "Brooke, I've been doing knots for a while so let me give it a crack." She reluctantly handed over the shoe and I was able to undo the mess. Before long, the shoe was on her foot and she was out the door.

If only knots were reserved for shoelaces! But they aren't. We all have them in our lives . . . maybe it's a bad decision, a horrible mistake, a troubled relationship or a million other knotty, messy things. But untying knots is the Lord's specialty. We need to cast all of our knots His way because He's been doing knots for a while. Psalm 55 invites us to heave it all His way. The question is: Will we?

"Cast your burden on the Lord [releasing the weight of it] and He will sustain you . . . " (Psalm 55:22 AMPLIFIED BIBLE). What a perfect picture of the benefits of *real* prayer! What have you been lugging around lately? What person or problem needs to be cast the Lord's way? What hurt, disappointment, worry, or disillusionment have you not released? We can't undo the knot and we can't continue to carry the burden. We must learn to cast each of them at the throne of grace where we will find our help in time of need.

- *Spend a moment talking to the Lord.*

- *Release the weight of _____ to Him.*

We must **come**, we must **cast**, and finally, we must **call**. What a privilege we have to call upon the name of the Lord and *know* that He hears. He is the God of the open ear:

I love the Lord, because He has heard [and now hears] my voice and my supplications. Because He has inclined His ear to me, therefore will I call upon Him as long as I live (Psalm 116:1-2 AMPLIFIED BIBLE).

We must call out to the God who hears! As believers we can talk with God at all times. We don't need to be in a church or even in a quiet place. And since we know that God hears and answers prayer (John 15: 7; 1 John 5:15-16), we *must* pray for our spouses, our children, our pastors, the ministry opportunities that come our way, as well as all the dramas and traumas that swirl around our personal lives. I have prayed through the Proverbs every year, claiming various Scriptures for my children, Bryan and Brooke. During Bryan's senior year in college he asked me to show him the Scriptures that I've prayed for him. It was a joy to show him the verses throughout my Bible that had "B & B" by them. And now I add an "A" for our dear daughter-in-law Alison.

How specifically do we pray? Are we using the promises of God as the basis of our prayers for ourselves and others? In my journal I write down the various Scriptures I am praying for my children, my husband, friends, etc. As we pray specifically we will be more aware of how God specifically answers. When we call out to God with our deepest concerns it cultivates intimacy in our walk with Him. Psalm 18 is a beautiful picture of King David calling out to God in a time of real trouble. In verse 3 he said, "I call to the LORD, who is worthy of praise, and I am saved from my enemies." And then in verses 16-19 we hear what God did in answer to David's plea,

> He [God] reached down from on high and took hold of me; he drew me out of deep waters. He rescued me from my powerful enemy, from my foes, who were too strong for me. They confronted me in the day of my disaster,

Avenue to
Intimacy

Following Him

When I Can't See
the End of the Road

208

but the LORD was my support. He brought me out into a spacious place; *he rescued me because he delighted in me.*" (Italics added.)

God came to his aid because He delighted in His son—just as He delights in us. When we call to Him we are demonstrating our dependence. Again, this breeds authentic intimacy with God. Remember the definition of intimacy? "A close, familiar, usually affectionate or loving personal relationship; a close association or detailed knowledge or deep understanding; the quality of being comfortable, warm or familiar." As we come to Him, **cast** our concerns and **call** upon His name, then our journey down the Avenue to Intimacy will be accelerated.

- *Pinpoint if you need to ask God to help you to come, call or cast.*

- *Reconsider the definition of intimacy, and choose a phrase you'd most like to be true of your prayer life.*

DISRUPTING INTIMACY

We've looked at three ways that our prayer life can grow. But what are some reasons it falls apart? There are as many excuses for not praying as there are people reading this book. The fact of the matter is that prayer is hard work. Why? Because it's so complicated? Because it takes great maturity? Or perhaps because prayer is only for the super-spiritual? No on each count. Prayer is hard because it goes against our natural desire to be in control of everything and to assume we know what's best.

- *Identify the main reasons you don't pray.*

We will cover three roadblocks to prayer: **sin, busyness,** and **spiritual battle**. The first way our intimacy can be disrupted is by sin. Unconfessed **sin** derails prayer faster than anything. When we know there are actions or attitudes in our lives that are displeasing to God, we must deal with them first. Psalm 66:18 says, "If I had cherished sin in my heart, the Lord would not have listened . . .."

• *Is sin choking out your prayer life?*

Another reason we get detoured in our prayer life is that we are too **busy**. Our families, friends, jobs, errands, soccer tournaments, TV and laziness can wreak havoc on our prayer time. Ruth Harms Calkin articulates this dilemma:

My dear, frenzied friend—
How I ache for her, Lord.
I just can't believe
How busy she is.

She eats so fast
Scolds so loudly
Clings so tight
Complains so bitterly
Worries so intensely
Rushes so wildly
Shops so impulsively
Plans so fearfully
Panics so frequently
Shatters so utterly.

No wonder she insists
There is no time to pray.

(*Tell Me Again, Lord, I Forget*)

Avenue to
Intimacy

Following Him

When I Can't See
the End of the Road

210

• *List the activities that keep you from prayer.*

The third way our intimacy with the Lord can be disrupted is through **spiritual battle.** If the enemy of our soul, Satan, can't keep us out of God's kingdom, then he'll go to plan B and focus on rendering us ineffective as believers. One way he does that is to keep us from praying. Have any of the following things happened to you? Suddenly, you are overcome with incredible fatigue as you begin your prayer time, or you just cannot concentrate on what you are praying about. Maybe you have an uncontrollable urge to clean out your desk or finish your "to do" list. Silly as these excuses may appear, they are stumbling blocks for most of us. Really, everything I've mentioned in this section can be a part of **spiritual warfare.** Sin and **busyness** both have the enemy's fingerprints on them. Why? Because each keeps us from praying and, as we've already seen, prayer develops a closer walk with the Lord. So if you want your prayer life to go deeper, begin by putting on the full armor of God as listed in Ephesians 6:10-18. Be vigilant in your struggle to make prayer a significant part of your life. Staying alert to sin, busyness and the enemy's schemes will be crucial as we venture down the Avenue to Intimacy.

• *Think through how the enemy has sabotaged your prayer life.*

ESTABLISHING INTIMACY

Very practically, how do we take the first step on the road to a powerful prayer life? What do we say and where do we begin? The disciples asked a very similar question after they'd followed the Lord for about a year and a half. In Luke 11:1 they asked Jesus, "Lord, teach us to pray." I have adopted that request as my own: "Lord, teach *me* to pray!" The two places that have been most helpful to me on my personal prayer journey are the Psalms and the Lord's Prayer.

- *Stop and pray Luke 11:1 for yourself.*

The Psalms form the longest book in the Bible. There are 150 chapters devoted to prayer. They were written by a variety of authors for the purpose of praising God. I have identified what I call the "psalmist pattern." A psalm often begins with praise, includes specifics on how the writer feels (joy, anger, hate, discouragement, loneliness, hope, dread, etc.), and ends with praise because the author has brought the character and promises of God to bear on his emotions or circumstances.

I've found only one psalm that doesn't include praise, Psalm 88. The Psalms give us permission to be honest with God as to what is going on in our lives. They teach us how to pray, what words to use and the importance of including praise every time we talk to the Lord. Begin with Psalm 1 and pray through one psalm a day. Here is how it works: Read a verse or two and then turn it into your own personal prayer back to the Lord. For example, Psalm 62:1 says, "My soul finds rest in God alone; my salvation comes from him." Your prayer back to the Lord could be, "Lord, I have a hard time finding my rest in you alone. I want my circumstances to be perfect before I can rest in You. Forgive me, Lord. Thank You for my wonderful salvation! What a mess I'd be without You as my God." Then go on to the next verse. The Lord will teach you how to pray as you use His Word as your prayer book.

The Lord's Prayer teaches us many wonderful lessons as well. It is found in Matthew 6:9-13 and Luke 11:2-4. This prayer emphasizes the praise of God, our commitment to do the will of God, the provision of God for our daily needs, His forgiveness for our many blunders, and God's protection from the evil one. This is stem-to-stern praying. Jesus said, "This, then, is how you should pray . . . " (Matthew 6:9). I don't think that means that this is the only prayer we can pray, but it does make clear what ingredients need to be included in our prayers.

These are a few insights on what to say when we pray, but where do we begin? First of all, set aside a specific time to pray each day. Pick a time where you *hope* to be alone and are most alert. Secondly, choose a place that will become your prayer spot. Third, always have your Bible with you and open it to a psalm or another portion of Scripture. Other good resources may include a hymnbook or a book with written prayers . . . anything that will help you focus your heart and mind on the Lord. Resources I've used over the years include:

- *Come Away, My Beloved* by Frances J. Roberts
- *Valley of Vision (A Collection of Puritan Prayers)* edited by Arthur Bennett
- *My Utmost for His Highest* by Oswald Chambers
- *Breakfast for the Soul* compiled by Judith Couchman
- *Daily with the King* by Glyn Evans
- *Prayer Portions* by Sylvia Gunter
- *Prayer Essentials, Volumes 1 & 2* by Sylvia Gunter
- *Amazing Grace* by Kenneth W. Osbeck
- *Prayers from the Heart* by Richard J. Foster

Along with set times of prayer, there are spontaneous times when we are praying in our heart as we go through our days. This is a "pray continually" kind of praying (see 1 Thessalonians 5:17) that keeps the Lord a part of all we do . . . and it will ensure that we stay motoring down the Avenue to Intimacy with vim and vigor.

- ***Select the Psalms or the Lord's Prayer as a place to begin deepening your walk with the Lord.***

- *Decide if you'd like to acquire a new companion book to enhance your prayer time.*

Avenue to
Intimacy

Following Him

When I Can't See
the End of the Road

213

The story is told of a man who'd traveled extensively down the Avenue to Intimacy. He was quickly approaching the end of his life. A priest went to visit him in the hospital and noticed an empty chair beside his bed. The priest asked if someone had been by to visit. The old man smiled and said with a twinkle in his eye, "I place Jesus on that chair, and talk to Him." The priest didn't understand, so the man explained, "Many years ago a friend told me that prayer was as simple as talking to a good friend. So, every day I just pull up a chair, invite Jesus to sit down, and then we have a heart-to-heart talk." A few days later the old man's daughter paid a visit to that same priest to inform him that her father had died. "Because he was so content," she explained, "I left him alone in his room for just a few hours. When I went back to his room he was dead. But what I can't understand is that his head was not on the pillow but on an empty chair beside his bed." (As told by Brennan Manning at U.S. Staff Conference, Campus Crusade for Christ, 1999)

This is a wonderful story of a person who didn't just imagine Jesus but experienced Jesus. Prayer has the power to lift us from a distant or formal relationship toward intimacy with the God who has so perfectly loved us.

CONCLUSION

Following Him is the greatest adventure anyone could experience. The promise of His guidance and love will always be demonstrated as we walk down each avenue.

Learning to follow the leading of the Holy Spirit will bring
complete satisfaction, and the intimacy to be realized will be the
sustaining force in your life.

Follow on, dear one, even if you can't see the end of the road,
because one day we will see His eyes sparkle and His lips move
and His voice say, 'Welcome Home My beloved, My bride.'

> *How lovely is your dwelling place,*
> *O LORD Almighty!*
> *My soul yearns, even faints,*
> *for the courts of the LORD.*
> *My heart and my flesh cry out*
> *for the living God.*
> *Better is one day in your courts*
> *than a thousand elsewhere;*
> *I would rather be a doorkeeper in the house of my God*
> *than dwell in the tents of the wicked.*
> *For the LORD God is a sun and shield;*
> *the LORD bestows favor and honor;*
> *no good thing does he withhold*
> *from those whose walk is blameless.*
> *O LORD Almighty,*
> *blessed is the man who trusts in you.*

(Psalm 84:1-2; 10-12)

Meditations for the Journey
INTIMACY

Consider . . .

God's Word

You hear, O LORD, the desire of the afflicted; you encourage them, and you listen to their cry . . .

Psalm 10:17

And I heard a loud voice from the throne saying, "Now the dwelling of God is with men, and he will live with them. They will be his people, and God himself will be with them and be their God. He will wipe every tear from their eyes. There will be no more death or mourning or crying or pain, for the old order of things has passed away."

Revelation 21:3-4

God's Heart

So come to Me as the child you are. Children, though they do ask Me why (and so will you), come to Me to crawl up on My lap and be near Me. They come to Me for love, not answers. If you come for answers, you will go away sad. If you come for love, you will be filled. To know the love of God, which surpasses all understanding—that is what I desire for you.

Ruth Senter, *Longing for Love*

*Meditations
for the Journey
Intimacy*

Following Him

*When I Can't See
the End of the Road*

216

 *Singing* . . .

What a Friend We Have in Jesus

*What a Friend we have in Jesus, all our sins and griefs to bear!
What a privilege to carry everything to God in prayer! O what
peace we often forfeit, O what needless pain we bear, all because
we do not carry everything to God in prayer.*

*Have we trials and temptations? Is there trouble anywhere?
We should never be discouraged—take it to the Lord in prayer.
Can we find a Friend so faithful who will all our sorrows share?
Jesus knows our every weakness—take it to the Lord in prayer.*

*Are we weak and heavy laden, cumbered with a load of care?
Precious Savior, still our refuge—take it to the Lord in prayer.
Do thy friends despise, forsake thee? Take it to the Lord in
prayer; in His arms He'll take and shield thee—thou wilt find
a solace there.*

Joseph Scriven, 1819-1886

 *Praying* . . .

*Your Word invites me to draw near to You, Great God, and so
I come—overloaded with my burdens, my broken dreams and
my failures. I am so thankful that You are a God who loves me
and wants me even when I am dirty and in desperate need of
the cleansing offered through the blood of the Lamb. Cleanse
me now, O God. Draw me closer and take me deeper still in
my relationship with You. Please, don't allow me to settle for
mediocre when You offer me Your all.* **Amen. Amen.**